The New Teacher's Survival Guide

By

Alex Boyle

Cover and images by

Violette Chenais

For those who inspire in the classroom

Contents

Figures

Introduction

So, you want to be a teacher? That's good! Teaching is one of the most rewarding and satisfying careers out there. It can also be one of the most challenging. Around 15% of newly qualified teachers leave teaching after their first year, and 35% don't last five years in the profession[1]. Not only that, but retention rates are worsening, not improving- a newly qualified teacher starting today is much less likely to still be teaching in five years' time than a teacher who qualified a decade ago[2]. Why is this? Is it money? Is it paperwork? Is it senior leadership? Is it…and whisper this… the children? The truth is, it's an amalgamation of all of these things and more. But don't panic! The New Teacher's Survival Guide is here you guide you around the pitfalls and difficulties many new teachers find themselves in, to remind you why you wanted to be a teacher in the first place, and reassure you that, with a little perseverance, some hard work (no-one said this would be easy!), and just a smidgen of good luck, teaching can be the best job in the world!

[1] HM Government. (2022) *School workforce in England*. Available at: https://explore-education-statistics.service.gov.uk/find-statistics/school-workforce-in-england#releaseHeadlines-dataBlock-1
[2] Education Executive. (2019) *Retention rate for teachers worsens*. Available at: https://edexec.co.uk/retention-rate-for-teachers-worsens/

I'm going to ask you a question, and it might be the most important question (and answer) in this whole book. It might be the most important question and answer in your entire teaching career: Why did you want to become a teacher?

Don't answer too quickly. Think about it. Had you worked with young people in some capacity before? Have you always gotten satisfaction from helping others learn something new, and develop, and grow? Did you just think the holidays sounded good? You might have been told you're not allowed to think that last one (you definitely are – but it might be worth considering now how much of that holiday time is entirely yours, and how much of it will be spent marking and planning. See: **Holidays**). Whatever your reason, write it down. Now. Preferably on a piece of card, a nice colourful piece if you have one, and keep it somewhere safe. I keep mine in my inside coat pocket. That's your reason for getting into teaching, and it is now also an incredibly important tool for you to use going forward. I'm not here to scare you, I love teaching, and I genuinely think it's the best job in the world, but I'd be lying if I said it wasn't sometimes hard. It's not unusual, especially in the early years, to go home thinking: 'That's it. I'm done. I'm not coming in tomorrow'. It's not unusual to cry. Schools can be hard places to work, sometimes we as teachers work ourselves too hard, push ourselves too far, and the effort we put in, the way we pour ourselves into our roles, isn't always fully appreciated. But when you do reach that point. When you feel you've put in all that you can, and you can't quite remember why you've done so- read the card. Remember why you got into teaching, and remember that you truly are making a difference, changing lives, and giving young people an opportunity that they wouldn't have otherwise. Some people take teachers for granted, they shouldn't, but they do. But think back a hundred years. It might feel a long time, but it really isn't (I'm a geography teacher by trade, and any geography teacher worth their salt will assure you, in terms of our planet, a hundred years is a blink of an eye. We work in geological timeframes of thousands of years, through which rivers carve valleys and glaciers flatten mountaintops), and think about the state of teaching in this country then. The Education Act of 1918 raised the school leaving age to 14[3], but in reality, many children still left at 13, or 12, if they ever went to school at all. Most left education without any formal qualifications and took manual industrial jobs with poor working conditions. A job in an office, or a shop floor, was a pipe dream for many, and university was an opportunity only for the very wealthy. A lot is said about our modern society, and it absolutely isn't perfect, but opportunities for young people now are undeniably more plentiful than they have been for most (arguably all) of British history, and in many other countries around the globe. And although social development has come in many forms, a large part of this is thanks to quality teachers. The people at the front of the classroom who don't give up, who nurture and educate young people, and who give them the tools to succeed in life. Even if you boiled it down to solely monetary terms, and we offer so much more, if you consider the economic impact of each of your students, throughout a long teaching career, as they earn qualifications, get jobs, start businesses, pay taxes, and even invent new things- the positive economic impact one teacher

---

[3] UK Parliament. (2022) *Education Act 1918*. Available at:
https://www.parliament.uk/about/living-heritage/transformingsociety/parliament-and-the-first-world-war/legislation-and-acts-of-war/education-act-1918/

has on this country, and perhaps globally, may well reach into the millions, if not the millions of millions.

You, as a teacher, are changing lives, and you are changing the world, and you must never, ever, forget that.

The New Teacher's Survival Guide will help you navigate your early years of teaching, through your trainee year, ECT (early career teacher) years, and beyond. And, as the world of teaching is constantly changing and evolving, there might even be some tips and tricks in here for teachers who are a bit longer in the tooth as well!

This guide is broken down into three main sections: The Students, The School, and The Rest. It is only by becoming competent in all three of these areas can we truly become effective, inspiring, super-teachers. But what do these headings mean?

The Students: This section will cover the most important element found in any school: The students. The reason we have a job, the people we should always have at the forefront of our minds, whether we're teaching, planning, or marking, and the people we *really* work for. But before we can plan effective lessons for them, we need to build relationships with the young people in our classrooms. We need to get to know them well enough that we can teach to their ability, in ways which will engage them, and stay on top of any potential behaviours.

The School: This section is all about the day-to-day of working in a school environment. Planning lessons, looking at the importance of including starters, main tasks, and plenaries. How to effectively include differentiation and utilise assessment, and how to build bridges between the school and home lives of our students.

The Rest: And then there's just the small matter of... everything else! For anyone entering a school environment, you will quickly come to appreciate one thing as a hard truth of teaching- working in schools means dealing with 'the rest'. There is plenty more to teaching than the students and the day-to-day role of planning, teaching, and marking. We'll discuss holiday time, what you're entitled to and how best to use it, the Teacher Standards, what they are and how they'll impact you, and most importantly, safeguarding and disclosures.

The Students

At what age is the human brain fully developed? At birth? 6 months? 5? 10? 18? Want to guess again? According to neuroscience, it's 25 at the earliest[4]. Not only are the young people you are working with not yet fully developed human beings, neither are many trainee or newly qualified teachers.

This puts us in a difficult situation. How can one teacher, at the start of their career, be expected to manage a group of thirty, maybe more, undeveloped brains; young people who, by the very definition may act immaturely, or impulsively, or overtly emotionally, or who may just get a kick out of being distracting and from disrupting your lessons? It's not an easy task, but take solace, you will be able to control your classes, and you will get them to thrive in your classroom. And, when you do feel confident in managing your classroom, and directing and teaching your students, you will have gained the most important ability you need to succeed in teaching. Knowing how to navigate your wider school (lesson planning, assessments, whole-school policies) and 'The Rest' (all the other things that will crop up), are all very important – but your main priority as a teacher, and never forget this, is your class and your students. Before we can plan our lessons and actually begin to *teach*, we need to consider our relationship with our

---

[4] Romer, D., Reyna, V., and Satterthwaite, T. (2017) Beyond stereotypes of adolescent risk taking: Placing the adolescent brain in developmental context. *Developmental Cognitive Neuroscience*. 27, p.19-34

students, and how we can build a classroom environment where everyone is happy, content and ready to learn. How do we achieve this? Read on, and discover, how to crack the most important aspect of teaching – The Students.

Setting Out Your Stall

Almost all teachers have heard the phrase, 'Don't smile until Christmas', or some variation of it. This used to be a key piece of advice imparted to new teachers at the start of their careers, and is still something banded about at many schools up and down the country today. The idea is that a teacher, with a new class starting in September, shouldn't smile or show any affection…or 'weakness', to their new students for the entirety of the autumn term. They should be strict. A disciplinarian. And this will show the class who is boss, and that no nonsense is allowed in their classroom. This advice, of course, is absolute drivel.

Working with a new class is about building relationships, between both students and teachers, and students and students, and setting out what **you** believe are acceptable standards in your classroom.

If we can wring out some element of sense from 'Don't smile until Christmas', it is this: **Perseverance**. One must be dedicated to not allow the slightest of smirks to grace their face for a four-month period, and although I actively encourage you to smile in your classroom, I do equally encourage you to persevere and be consistent with your classroom standards. The work you put in during that first term, encouraging what you deem to be acceptable behaviours, and picking up on instances of less desirable behaviours, will make your life far easier in terms 2 and 3, and for the rest of your time teaching at that school. It is important you set out your stall from day one, so that there is no confusion in your classroom as to what your expectations are. I can't promise these expectations will always be followed, but as long as everyone knows what is and isn't acceptable, praise and consequences can be dished out consistently and fairly when standards and expectations are, or are not, met. Remember what I said about your students not having fully developed brains yet? One thing they will crave is consistent and fair rules[5]. This isn't to say your students aren't incredibly bright, young academic minds, but they will want to know, in very plain and simple terms, what your expectations are. If one day you pick up on a student for wearing trainers instead of school shoes, but then the very next day you don't pick up on another student for doing exactly the same thing, you will cause a rift, and you will suddenly find you have more students pushing the boundaries, and wearing trainers in this instance, because they don't see a consistent and fair approach on picking them up for it. The next time you do ask a student why they have turned up in bright white Air Jordans, you can expect a response of: 'But you let so-and-so wear their trainers yesterday!' What do you do here? Do you consequence one student but not the other? Do you let this student off today, to make things even? Do you retrospectively consequence the student who is currently making the right decision, and is wearing school shoes, for wearing trainers in the past? None of these are good options, and

---

[5] Newport Academy. (2021) *Why Teens Need Rules: How Parents Can Support Both Independence and Structure.* Available at:
https://www.newportacademy.com/resources/mental-health/why-teens-need-rules/

you've got yourself into a pickle. And why are you in a pickle? Because you didn't properly set out your stall, and you weren't consistent in enforcing your own classroom standards.

Now here's where I'm supposed to list what your classroom standards should be, right? Do these things and a calm, happy, productive classroom, you will receive. Unfortunately, it doesn't work that way. Every classroom will be different, and expectations will vary from school to school. Often, many of the standards you will enforce will be directed by your school and their whole-school policies. Even if you have 'free reign' within your classroom, you will find appropriate rules and standards will differ from school to school, even from classroom to classroom, and throughout your teaching career. In one school, uniform may be strictly enforced (coincidently, there is conflicting research on whether wearing a uniform improves behaviour, attendance and results[6] [7]), while in another school, just getting a student into school and participating in lessons may be a huge achievement, and whether they're wearing a uniform or a tracksuit may be the least of your concerns.

By setting out your stall early, you are aiming to gain one thing: A reputation. Tell me now, what was Pablo Escobar like? A larger than life, drug-fuelled psychopath? A man who made so much money he didn't know what to do

---

[6] Ansari, A., Shepard, M., and Gottfried, M. (2022) School uniforms and student behavior: is there a link? *Early Childhood Research Quarterly*. 58 (1), p.278-286
[7] Education Endowment Foundation. (2021) *School uniform*. Available at: https://educationendowmentfoundation.org.uk/education-evidence/teaching-learning-toolkit/school-uniform

with it, and someone who also wouldn't think twice about bludgeoning a man to death if they got in his way? Now, what about Mahatma Gandhi? A calm, peaceful man? A man who campaigned for Indian independence, who worked tirelessly to bring more equality to the people of his country, and who promoted love and respect? How do you know? Have you ever met Escobar of Gandhi? It's very unlikely. However, you have heard of their **reputation**. My descriptions of the pair may not even be entirely correct, I am by no means a historian (although I have found myself teaching History in the past!). But I do know how they are both perceived in modern society, because their reputations proceed them.

By setting out your stall in your classroom, you will also build a reputation. New students coming through will hear of these reputations, and if it is well known around the school that 'Sir' or 'Mrs' expects their first lesson to start at 9:00 am sharp, and that anyone dawdling in after 9:01 am will make the time back at break or lunch, you will find students will make it to your classroom on time, and behaviours very well may improve. Similarly, if there is a reputation that you do not follow through with consequences, or you do not pick up on certain behaviours, you will find students will push the boundaries and find out just how much they can get away with.

A last, very important thing to remember, is that reputations are like first impressions, you can only make one, and they tend to stick. Coming back after Christmas, thinking you can set out your stall and win back students who have already built a perception of you, is very difficult. Often, you will find that ship has already sailed and that there will be a palpable resistance against any new standards and expectations you try to introduce. Do yourself a favour and decide before September what you feel is and isn't acceptable in your classroom, and make these clear from day one. This is easier said than done, and we all make mistakes in our early teaching careers – but make these mistakes during your training placements. Learn from them. And then go into that first ECT position with a plan in mind.

Now, about this plan...

Consistency. Consistency. Consistency. And Fairness.

I can't tell you exactly what standards and expectations to expect and instil in your classroom, but here are some suggestions which have worked well for me in the past (as always, the appropriateness of these will vary depending on the school you find yourself in and the particular sets of students you have in your classes, in that school. Utilise your own teacher judgement when deciding which standards and expectations are best suited):

- **Punctuality** – Do you want to be a teacher whose lessons start *exactly* on the hour? This can be a good way to ensure students arrive promptly and with a positive attitude to start their learning. Wasting 5 minutes at the start and end of each lesson, regularly, will add up to hours by the end of the year.

- **Attitudes to Learning** – A positive and proactive attitude to learning might be paramount in your classroom. You may expect students to come into your room, independently get their book out, copy down a date and title from the board, and begin their starter. Those who do, are rewarded. Those who don't, are reminded.

- **Uniform** – One which is more likely to be whole-school driven, but perhaps you want to be a stern enforcer of uniform policies. If this is whole-school, all teachers should, of course, be enforcing the same, and pulling in the same direction. This lessens the dreaded cries of, 'But Sir/Miss let me wear these!'

- **Attitude and Manners** – Here's one I do recommend, in any school. Manners, as they say, cost nothing, and everyone in your classroom, students and staff, should be able to talk to each other in a polite and respectful way. Reward good examples and promote achievable targets: Waiting patiently with hands raised rather than shouting out, asking to be excused to use the toilet, rather than just walking out, and using appropriate language. Try to create a classroom which is a pleasant environment to be, and learn, in.

Whatever you choose to implement in your classroom, there are two key things you must remember: Fairness and Consistency. Young people crave fairness[8]. If you try to enforce rules which students can't understand or don't see as fair, you will find there will be resistance (there may also be resistance to entirely fair and reasonable rules, those that are in place to keep students

---

[8] Smith. L., Todd. L., and Lang. K. (2017) Students' views on fairness in education: the importance of relational justice and stakes fairness. *Research Papers in Education*. 33 (3), p.336-353

safe or allow them to concentrate on their learning, but that is, as they say, an occupational hazard).

The best method to ensure rules are seen as fair by your student population? Make them together. When teaching a new class for the first time, it is highly recommended that you take ten minutes as a whole class to decide and agree on some ground rules. By all means get the ball rolling, but don't dictate all the rules here, all the things you think make up a perfect classroom. You want active participation, so that later on, if standards and expectations are not being met, you can refer back to the 'Classroom Rules', which you **all** formed and agreed on together in a fair and democratic manner (and as with all democracies, some animals are more equal than others, and you very may steer some of the rulemaking in your favour- but don't be too blunt about this). You ideally want students putting their hands up and suggesting, 'We all put our hands up rather than shout out', and, 'We are all polite and respectful of each other in this classroom'. If you are finding this hard to achieve, start by suggesting one rule of your own, asking students if they agree this would be fair and sensible, and then asking students to suggest theirs. You may need to pick one or two students to begin with, but soon ideas will start to flow. Once these rules have been agreed on, take the time to write them up and display them prominently on the classroom wall. This will go a huge way to stopping your classroom from being a 'Teacher vs Students' environment, and instead help build a shared environment of agreed standards and expectations, which has been designed for everyone to reach their best outcomes.

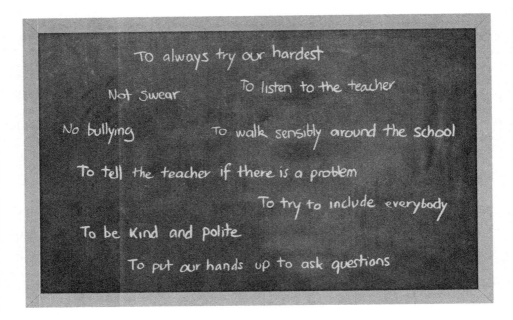

Figure 1 - Agreed Classroom Rules

Consistency. Once you have your classroom ground rules, you need to enforce them: **Consistently**. One way to quickly lose a class is to be inconsistent, to pick up on one student for a certain behaviour, but then to allow others to get away with the exact same thing. I can't repeat this enough: Be consistent. Once you set your classroom expectations, ensure everyone is aware of them and follows them. This applies for you as well! If you set a five-minute lunch detention, be consistent and follow it up. Be there, do the five minutes. Build your teacher reputation. If you don't, and if you set things or make promises that aren't fulfilled, you will quickly build the exact type of school reputation you're trying to avoid.

Consistency doesn't just mean ruling your classroom with an iron fist either, picking up on every little behaviour, every time. Be consistent with praise. Tell every student who produces a good piece of work how brilliant they are, have a 'Star Chart' on the wall that you add stars to, on a regular and consistent basis. Students crave praise, and they need to know it is forthcoming from you and how they can get it. Be consistent with everything, but especially with your praise.

Building Relationships

You are **not** your students' friend. The idea that you can or should be your students' friend is a misconception that some trainee teachers have when starting their careers, and it's one you need to banish quickly. I wouldn't recommend revealing too much about your personal life (favourite sports teams or films: Yes. Mother's maiden name and birthplace: No), and **don't even think of adding or accepting friend requests on social media**. This can quickly land you in hot water, and at its very least, is highly unprofessional.

You want you gain your students' respect. But this doesn't mean they can't also like you, and that you cannot like them. An open secret within teaching circles: We do all have our favourite students. And that's fine. And building relationships, and getting on well with students whom you spend potentially hours and hours with each week, is a good thing. They just aren't your friends. Think of the relationships you are building in the classroom as platonic co-worker relationships that you'd find in any office setting. You want to get on with the people who spend a lot of time in your general vicinity, you may even grow to like each other, but that doesn't mean you want to meet and have a coffee with them at the weekend.

So how to build these relationships? You find common ground. School is, of course, about gaining academic results and growing young people into young professionals who can survive and thrive in the workplace. But it's also so much more. And growing socially, developing relationships, and, frankly, learning how to make adult small talk, are all part of this. My recommendation, any school that discourages you from making small talk with your students, at appropriate times (during form periods, or while worksheets are being handed out), isn't a school you want to be spending an extended period of time at, and trust me, these schools do unfortunately exist. But let's say you're at a good school, with a headteacher who encourages holistic social development, what can you discuss? That comes down to you. Students, and their interests, have moved on since you were in school; this I can guarantee, even if you've only been out of the education system for a few short years yourself. I have found in my own experience that there is now a huge interest in social media stars. People who are famous on Youtube or Tik Tok. People I, frankly, know zilch about. Maybe you know a bit more about social media than I do (and ever will), and can join in with these conversations. But, if you can't, don't fear! The usual water cooler topics of sports, music, and simply whatever was on the telly last night, can still suffice. I like to have these conversations first thing in the morning, as students come into my room. These are a great opportunity to greet the students, check on their wellbeing (in a low-key way), and start them off on the right foot for the day[9]. Don't be afraid to find out more about the lives of your students either. I've advised you not to share too much, but your students may be willing to share. What did they have for dinner last night? Are they involved in any clubs or sports? Do they have brothers and sisters? Be mindful of what you ask, you're making conversation, not interrogating, but also listen to what you find out. Do you hear something to suggest a home life isn't so good? Note this down, any concerns will need reporting. More on this in: **Safeguarding**.

Learning The Names

One thing you'll absolutely need to do straight away when starting with a new class is learn your students' names. It sounds obvious, just good manners, right? And sometimes it's easy, but not always. I'd never had a problem learning and remembering names until I started my first teaching job. In a big school, it's very possible you will teach about ten different classes per week, maybe more. If in each class you have thirty students, congratulations, you are now responsible for three-hundred young people and have three-hundred names to remember. It won't be long until you're Head of Year, or Head of Department, and then you'll have even more to learn.

My first school was in an inner-city area with high levels of international immigration, and a large Islamic population. I'd grown up in an area with very low levels of both, out in the country. I knew what the student population of my new school entailed, so this wasn't a surprise, but it wasn't

---

[9] Johnson, B., and Bowman, H. (2021). *Dear Teacher*. Routledge: Abingdon-on-Thames

until I started that I realised most of the names I would have to learn were names I'd never heard before in my life. There were sounds within the names I didn't associate with the letters used. You may be more enlightened than I was at the time, but I didn't realise 'aa' in many names with middle eastern origins makes an 'ar' sound, or that a 'q', without a 'u' anywhere in sight, is sometimes pronounced as an 'x', such as the name Aqa being pronounced 'Axa'. To a room full of teenagers, pronouncing Aqa like 'Aqua' is apparently the funniest thing imaginable, and can lead to initial difficulties in building those classroom relationships. It can also be embarrassing, or even insulting, to the individual. We all like our names to be spelt and pronounced correctly.

There's no getting around it, you need to learn the names. You can't expect a student to respect, or like, you, if you can't remember their name. Forgetting a name is a quick way to becoming a student's least favourite teacher. It's also a truth that the names of your highest achievers and naughtiest students will stick in your mind first. In many classrooms, up and down the country, there is a forgotten middle section. A group of well-behaved, quiet, middling students, who get easily overlooked while teachers deal with the behaviours and needs of others. Do not become one of these teachers with a forgotten middle section. You owe it to your students to offer your best practice to both the most needy, behavioural-challenged, students, and to the most quiet, independent ones. And, to all the students in between. Learn all of their names, and (attempt) to build relationships with every last one of them. They're the reason you're in a job, after all.

Some helpful tips: Don't be shy about the fact you don't know all their names Day 1. But be clear you will learn. I often say, when taking a new class's register for the first time, 'Apologies in advance if I mispronounce any names, please correct me, and I'll try to get them right next time'. Make a joke about it, 'I'm old and forgetful', or, 'Ooh, I was closer that time'. But do learn the names. Humour will show you're human, and you're trying, but ultimately the students will want to know that you know who they are. Try to have all the names learnt by the end of your first week, two weeks at a push if you're new to a big school. Sometimes it *will* take longer, and don't beat yourself up about that, but keep going! You'll get there.

This brings me to the most important tip for learning names: Utilise your seating plans. When welcoming any new class into your classroom, have a seating plan prepared, and either have it on display on an interactive whiteboard, or, using your own hardcopy, direct each student to their new seat. You may get some resistance, 'I want to sit with so-and-so!', but resist this, and be persistent in (you guessed it) setting out your stall (consider also: building a reputation, classroom standards and expectations). Have a physical copy of this seating plan to hand. Many schools will have a program for you to build seating plans on, and to print out from (MegaSeatingPlan is one I'm familiar with), but if you need to do this by hand, do it. Another tip here, if you're making multiple seating plans for multiple classes, in the same classroom, sketch out your classroom tables once, and photocopy this blank plan of your room the adequate number of times. Then fill in for each class. Look at the plan in your hand, look up at your students. You have a plan of them all, in the correct seats (persevere, keep them in these seats, at least to begin with), with their names written on. When addressing the students, look down at your plan, and use their names. Practice makes perfect.

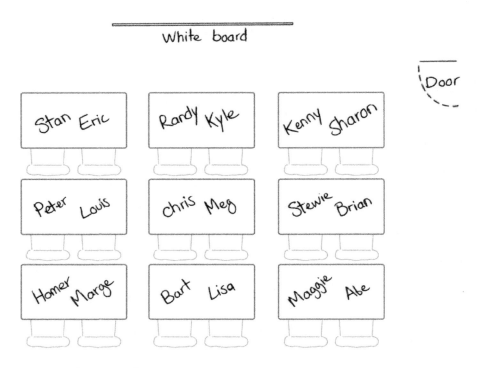

Figure 2- Example Seating Plan

Ice-breakers

When I get a new class and I want to start building relationships, I like to start with some ice-breakers. These are a great way to get to know your students and to begin to build those positive relationships, both between teacher and students and students and students.

Here are a few of my favourite ice-breaker games, and how to play them:

- **Two Truths and a Lie:** Ask each student to come up with three facts about themselves, two which are true, one which is false. Other students in the room should then ask follow-up questions to try and determine which fact is untrue.

- **The Line Order Game:** Ask all the students to get out of their seats and form a line (this may be best to do outside if you don't have the classroom space). Then, ask the students to get into certain orders, such as height order, age order, shoe size order, by the number of siblings they have (and any other orders you can think of). Don't help out the students, allow them to ask for their peers' birthdates or shoe sizes, as they try to sort themselves into the correct orders.

- **Sit Down If…:** Have the students form a circle, stood up, with you in the middle. Ask a series of Yes/No questions such as, 'Do you have any brothers or sisters?' or, 'Are you part of a sports club?' If a student can answer 'Yes' to any of your questions, they must sit down. The last student standing is the winner, and must give a fact about themselves they could have answered 'Yes' to, if asked, such as, 'Do you/I have a dog at home'.

- **Beachball Questions:** Blow up a beachball and write icebreaker questions in each of the sections around it. Questions such as, 'Do you have any pets?', 'What's your favourite colour?', or 'What's your favourite sports team?'. Have the class pass the beachball around, and at random intervals instruct them to stop. The student with the beachball in their hands must answer the question directly facing them.

- **Marooned on a Desert Island:** Put your students in groups of approx. 5. Each group has been marooned on a desert island, and can only use items on their person or from their bags to survive. Each member of the group must select one item (a group of 5 would have 5 items in total), and as a group they must explain why they have selected their items, and how they might help them to survive until help arrives.

Give these a go, and even come up with some of your own. The most important thing is that the students are interacting together, getting to know each other, and often working towards a common goal. And **don't** fall into the trap of thinking ice-breaker games are just for younger year groups, bigger kids also need these skills and will love joining in!

Behaviour

This guide is full of tips to help you navigate the early years of your teaching career, but young people can be unpredictable and you will, almost certainly, come across a time when you have followed all my tips, you've learnt the names, you've been fair and consistent, you've started to implement a reputation around the school, and you've done your best to build relationships within the classroom – and still a student is misbehaving in a way that seems utterly irrational to you.

Remember how our young peoples' brains are still in development? How about adding in SEND (Special Educational Needs and/or Disability) diagnoses, which can, amongst other things, make it harder for our young people to concentrate, stay on task, or even just feel comfortable in the classroom environment (just a quick caveat, although there are diagnoses which *can* have links with behaviour, I've taught hundreds of young people with additional SENDs who have been the nicest, most pleasant, young people you could ever wish to meet). What about problems at home? Being exposed to violence, drinking, or just an environment with little to no structure? The effects of puberty? How about, and sometimes we can forget this, that our young people are human, are developing, and might have just woken up on the wrong side of the bed that day? It's not to say any of these are *excuses*, but there are reasons why, even when you've done everything right, some students may display poor behaviour in your classroom.

So, what can you do about it? It's not easy, especially when you've planned a high-quality lesson, you've done all the right things, and a student, or group of students, decides they are going to take the opportunity to disrupt everything you've put in place (for them!). **Keep your cool**. This is, unfortunate as it may be, another occupational hazard of the job, and nine out of ten times it's not personal. It can be hard to believe, but often, if a student is misbehaving for you, they are also misbehaving for their other teachers. Ask your colleagues! Reassure yourself that the behaviour isn't personal towards you, and even better, see if your colleagues have put any strategies in place to help deal with a student's behaviour which you could also implement.

Be consistent. Even if it's seemingly not working, keep doing what you're doing. That's how we build expectations and standards. It's also how we communicate to the student(s) that we're being fair. It's the same expectations, the same rules, the same rewards, and the same sanctions and consequences, for the entire class. Day after day. These routines become normalised, and we can use them to teach what we consider appropriate behaviour in our classrooms[10]. Also, ensure you're being consistent and following-through with both the rewards and sanctions which you are setting following classroom behaviours. Setting a break-time detention and failing to turn up yourself, or promising a class treat which never materialises, is a quick way to show your students that your classroom rules won't be consistently enforced, and behaviour will start to deteriorate as boundaries are pushed without fear of comeuppance.

---

[10] Bennett, T. (2020) *Running the Room*. John Catt Educational LTD: London

Finally, **be confident in your school's behavioural policy**. If all else fails, be consistent with your school's behavioural policy, and be confident in what your options and next steps are. There is nothing worse than having a student misbehave in your room, from constant low-level disruption, to throwing chairs and picking fights, and thinking to yourself, 'I have no idea how to react'. Whatever the policy is, go into your classroom confident in what you need to do. Often this will be something along the lines of one verbal warning, followed by a formal warning on the board, a breaktime detention, and finally, if it has gotten to a level where a student is putting themselves or others at risk, calling for a member of SLT (Senior Leadership Team) or another designated member of staff to come and remove the student from your room. This may be followed up with an after-school detention, a suspension, or even an expulsion for repeat behaviour. Policy will vary from school to school, you just need to know, when all else seemingly has failed (and it will feel like this sometimes), what your next steps are. In schools with strong behaviour procedures, the behaviour policy should be consistent across the school and students should be clear on what is, and is not, acceptable behaviour. Ultimately, this will come down to your school and school leaders, who have a bigger impact on whole-school behaviour than individual teachers[11], but you should do your upmost to be knowledgeable of, and to follow thoroughly, whatever policy is put in place. What we do know is that schools with strong behavioural policies generally see improvement in whole-

---

[11] Bennett, T. (2017) *Creating a culture: how school leaders can optimise behaviour*. Available at:
https://assets.publishing.service.gov.uk/government/uploads/system/uploads/attachment_data/file/602487/Tom_Bennett_Independent_Review_of_Behaviour_in_Schools.pdf

school behaviour, and have, on average, improved student attainment and improved staff wellbeing and retainment[12]. Behaviour management is an important part of schooling and can make a huge impact on the quality of learning in our classrooms.

This is all well and good, but you're probably asking yourself, 'What practical measures can I take in my classroom to improve behaviour?' This is a difficult question. What works for one group of students, will not necessarily work for another. However, throughout my teaching career I have come across a few strategies which I have had successes with, which you may want to try out for yourself:

Seating Plans: I have already mentioned how seating plans are a great tool for helping you learn students' names, and how this can help you build positive relationships with new classes. This on its own can go a long way to improving behaviour – a student who knows you know them, and who may even start to like you because of this, can very well display more positive behaviours in your classroom (for some this may sound 'woolly', but consider that many behaviours are intrinsically linked to poor relationships elsewhere, such as at home, and that having positive relationships in school can offer a

---

[12] Bennett, T. (2017) *Creating a culture: how school leaders can optimise behaviour.* Available at:
https://assets.publishing.service.gov.uk/government/uploads/system/uploads/attachment_data/file/602487/Tom_Bennett_Independent_Review_of_Behaviour_in_Schools.pdf

student a whole new outlook on themselves and their relationships with others[13]).

In a more concrete sense, I often advise ECTs that behaviour management begins with seating plans, because this is how we arrange the personalities in our classrooms and keep certain students together or away from each other. Two chatty friends who, regularly, cannot bring themselves to end their break-time conversations? Place them on opposite sides of the room. A student at the back, thinking they can hide their antics, or that they can distract all the other students currently in their view? Move them to the front; now their peers are out of line-of-sight, and you've got eyes directly on them. Alternatively, a student who doesn't get on well with others on their table, won't join in with groupwork, and is displaying signs of low confidence? Try moving them to a table they'd work better on, with peers they get on better with.

Seating plans on their own won't always lead to calmer and more focused classrooms, but it is much easier to begin building the kind of classroom expectations, and ambience, you want, when you have organised the students within it.

Getting a Class Stood Up: Low -level class disruption is a tricky obstacle for any new teacher. It is often easier to deal with one student who has clearly broken the rules, than it is to deal with a chatty, unfocused, or disruptive class

---

[13] Chandler, L. K., & Dahlquist, C. M. (2015) *Functional assessment: Strategies to Prevent and Remediate Challenging Behavior*. 4th ed. Pearson: London.

who are bending the rules and pushing the boundaries of your expectations. With one student, you can follow the whole-school policy and usually come to some sort of conclusion – but it can be very difficult to give warnings to a whole class who are a bit too 'chatty'.

In these instances, instead of repeatedly asking a class to quieten down (especially when it hasn't worked, once, twice, three times…), ask them to stand up. Don't tell them why, count down from three, 'Three, two, one, and everybody stood behind their chairs please.' The quick change, and the confusion that goes along with it, can often instinctively quieten down a room, offering you the opportunity to either give the instruction you were unable to deliver previously, or, to give a firm but friendly warning, 'I shouldn't have to bring you all to your feet for the noise level to be acceptable in this room. Please keep the volume lower, and remember our hands up to speak rule'.

I would recommend only using this method periodically, as it may lose its emphasis if it becomes too commonplace and loses its 'confusion' aspect.

Post-it Notes: There are a couple different ways to utilise post-it notes to tackle low-level behaviours. If you've got a student who can't help but shout out in class, who just isn't complying with your hands up policy, give them three post-its at the start of the day. Each time the student shouts out, take one post-it away. At the end of the day, reward the student if there are still post-its left on their desk, or consequence if all three are gone.

Alternatively, you may have the problem of a student or students becoming lethargic, and not engaging with your lessons. In this case, give either the targeted group, or better yet, every student in the class, a post-it at the start of the day or lesson. When a student puts their hand up and answers a question correctly, take the post-it away. By the end of the lesson/day, all post-its must have been collected in. To be extra sustainable, playing cards can be used in place of single-use post-its.

Restorative Conversations: After a behaviour has taken place and school policy has been followed in terms of consequences and sanctions, it's a good idea to take the time to have a conversation with the offending student before you teach them again, especially if the sanctions involved removing them from your classroom.

As previously mentioned, students may act out and behave in inappropriate ways for a multitude of different reasons, and it can be hugely beneficial to try to get to the bottom of their reasoning before you teach the student again. This way we can try and put intervention and support in place to reduce repeat behaviour[14]. It's also a good idea to try and rebuild those relationships, because it doesn't matter how rational and fair you were – the majority of students who have been sanctioned, and removed from classrooms, will put some (if not all) of the blame on the teacher.

---

[14] Bennett, T. (2017) *Creating a culture: how school leaders can optimise behaviour.* Available at:
https://assets.publishing.service.gov.uk/government/uploads/system/uploads/attachmen t_data/file/602487/Tom_Bennett_Independent_Review_of_Behaviour_in_Schools.pdf.

Invite the student back to your room (or for those who won't accept this offer, go and see them during any detentions which followed the initial behaviour), and try to initiate a meaningful conversation to explore why the behaviours took place, how the student feels in your classroom, and what, from their perspective, could be changed to improve the way they feel in your lessons. These conversations can sometimes be tricky to navigate, especially for less experienced teachers, so don't fear asking a mentor or Head of Department to accompany you and help facilitate these meetings.

Routines: One of the biggest ways we can build expectations, training our students in the behaviours which we deem acceptable in our classroom, and which are also acceptable in the wider-world and which will help them holistically develop into respectable members of society (quite a heavy responsibility, when you stop and think about it), is to put in place proper routines. This very much links back to Consistency and Fairness, and as with instilling standards and expectations, we must be consistent and fair when introducing and following through with classroom routines. Consider having a different pair of students handing out the workbooks each lesson. If you make a rota, they can even get on with this routine independently without the need for your reminders. Introduce a routine of making sure desks are clean at the end of lessons, or that chairs are tucked away or put up on top of tables at the end of the day. Link in your routines with your expectations on attitude to learning; date and titles written down and starters attempted independently before you even begin delivering the learning. Routines built around checking or peer-assessing work, before you get around to a particular table or student, have even been shown to have positive impacts on attainment, as students are free to carry on and attempt the next task rather than waiting for your feedback[15].

Embedding these routines into your classroom will take time, and will require you, as the teacher, to be consistent in enforcing them[16]. But once they're fully in place, students will have a much better understanding of what is expected of them in your room and this in turn can impact the culture of your classroom and improve behaviours. Routines take time and effort to get right, but they're worth it.

When discussing behaviours, something intrinsically linked with negativity (whether or not this should be the case is very much up for debate), it's important to remember that in most schools in Britain (and largely worldwide), students displaying very poor behaviours are a minority. In my years of teaching I have only witnessed a handful of fights, which were broken up and dealt with quickly, have never had to have a student expelled, although there have been a couple of suspensions, and I always try to implement, and highly recommend, a culture of praising good work and behaviour in your classroom, with consequences and sanctions being a back-up. Behaviour will vary from school to school, and from class to class, but the vast majority of young people you will meet will be lovely and will appreciate the work you put in for them (even if they don't *always* tell you so). Knowing the behaviour

---

[15] Fiorella, L. (2020) 'The Science of Habit and Its Implications for Student Learning and Well-being'. *Educational Psychology Review*. 32 (1), pp. 603–625

[16] Bennett, T. (2020) *Running the Room*. John Catt Educational LTD: London

policy, and what to do if things do go wrong, is important for the rare times when things aren't going to plan.

The School

Now, you are in full control of your classroom (or on your way to getting there, at least). You are confident in building relationships, your own reputation, and creating an environment that will allow you to deliver a high standard of learning to your students. And you expect that your school will allow you to freely get on with this? Hold your horses there! And how do we deliver that learning, anyway? You may have mastered the students, but now you've got to deal with the next key element of teaching: The School.

Lesson Planning

High-quality lessons take place in the classroom, but they start long before that. They start with planning. Different schools will have different planning criterium, different elements that must (or must not) appear in lessons, and will ask for differing levels of evidence of planning. As much as I cannot give specific details as to what your school will require, I can (and will) break-down how I believe a good lesson can be structured, and offer resources and advice on how to plan high-quality lessons which put the learning at the forefront.

In doing so, we will need to consider our *pedagogy*. Our pedagogy is our teaching method, the act, both physical and mental, of taking a subject of information and imparting it to a class of students[17]. There are many different forms of teaching methods, and many different ways to break-down a lesson, with a range of activities and learning opportunities. Some will work fantastically for you, others may not gel well with your particular teaching style, but some aspects of a lesson are crucial (such as Learning Objectives) and will fit in with any and all pedagogies. When beginning to plan lessons at the start of your career, one of the most important pieces of advice I can offer you is this: Try out lots of different styles, methods and activities. Find out what works for you, and don't fear trying something new. It might just be what you were looking for, and it might just engage and inspire your students in a way you couldn't have expected.

So, how do we begin? Usually, with our Learning Objectives...

Learning Objectives: Why are you teaching the lesson you're teaching? And no, 'because it's on the curriculum' is not the correct answer. Your Religious Education curriculum may be telling you you've got to teach religious festivals, and this week you are supposed to be focusing on the festival of Diwali. So, in theory, you could stand at the front of the room and reel off fact after fact about what happens during Diwali, the festival of lights. You could even save yourself the time and effort and give each student a premade pack with all the information inside. But would this act of reading and

---

[17] Alexander, R. (2009) 'Towards a Comparative Pedagogy', in Cowen, R. and Kazamias, A. M. (eds) *International Handbook of Comparative Education*. Springer: London. pp. 923–942

memorising be beneficial for your students? And would they all be able to access this 'lesson'? Could you confidently say they have all *learnt* something? The answer, is no.

Why is it important to teach about religious festivals? Is it to grow tolerance and understanding of other cultures in our students? Is it to assist them in growing-up into global citizens who both understand and are accepting of other people's faiths around the world? Is it to introduce new ways of thinking? Maybe your student population is very Church of England? Or not religious at all? At no point should schools force religion on students, but I believe it is important to open our young peoples' eyes to others' ways of thinking and celebrating. Spiritual growth and wellbeing, and starting to think about our place in the world, are important aspects of any young person's development. My point is, your lessons are incredibly important tools which mould young minds, and you should know **why** you're teaching any particular lesson.

Once you are confident in the why, you need to consider what you want your students to achieve in your lesson. This leads us to your **Learning Objective**. A high-quality Learning Objective should be a clear, measurable, objective which leads to an outcome your students should have learnt or achieved by the end of your lesson. Lazy teachers often confuse Learning Objectives with 'titles'. Your LO is not your lesson title. Sticking with the Diwali theme, our lesson title may be something along the lines of: *The Festival of Diwali*. A good LO could be:

'To research the origins of the festival of Diwali, and to explore how the festival is celebrated around the world today.'

> **LO**: To **research** the *origins* of the festival of *Diwali*, and to **explore** <u>how the festival is celebrated around the world today</u>.
>
> **Command Words**
> *Focus*
> <u>Measurable Element</u>

Figure 3- Example Learning Objective

Bosh! Straight away, our students' learning is focused. They are focusing on the origins of the festival and the ways in which the festival is celebrated today. We've then added in some command words for good measure: *Research* and *Explore*. These gives clues to how the lesson's teaching and learning will take place. The research aspect may be computer-based, or through information packs spread around the room, whatever the method, the students will already begin to deduce that part of the lesson is based around their independent (or group) research and investigation. The second part of our LO, to explore how the festival is celebrated, may very well be teacher-led, with some form of work/assessment, such as worksheets or essay-style questions, used to assess the learning made. Our LO is measurable, and this is really important. You should be able to tell by the end of the session whether or not a student can say how the festival of Diwali is celebrated today. This doesn't mean the learning has to be quantitatively measurable (not always at least), and not every lesson needs to end with a quiz, marked to show how many answers the students can give on a particular topic. Yet, qualitatively, through discussion and the work in their books, you should be able to see if your students leave this lesson with an understanding of the origins of Diwali and the ways it is celebrated. If they can't, your LO may have not been met.

But how exactly are the students in this Religious Education lesson example researching and exploring Diwali? Here is where your Success Criteria come in. These are criterium your students must meet in order to achieve their LO. Quality SCs need to be specific – what *specifically* are you asking your students to do, to learn about Diwali and meet their LO? SCs in this example could be:

1. *To independently research the origins of Diwali using the computers, and to create a presentation on your findings.*
2. *To read the diary extract 'My Diwali' and to answer the comprehension questions focusing on how Diwali is celebrated today.*
3. *To use what you have learnt to answer the GCSE style question, 'Assess the ways in which the celebrations of Diwali and Hannukah both share similarities and have differences' (8 marks).*

When planning LOs and SCs early on in your teaching career, you may want to use WALT and WILF to help you (no, these aren't two blokes who will come in and write your learning objectives for you, unfortunately). WALT is an acronym for 'We Are Learning To', and in essence that's what a good LO will tell you – what the lesson's learning will be. WILF stands for 'What I'm Looking For', and these are the specific things you as the teacher will be looking for and expecting from your students within the lesson, as they work towards the overarching learning, not dissimilar to the specific SCs we'd expect students to meet. WALT and WILF are more commonly seen in primary education, but can still have their place in secondary. Either to bring some consistency to your students' learning, especially for year 7 students transitioning from primary to secondary, or just within your planning if they better help you visualise what aspects are required in strong LOs and SCs.

High-quality Learning Objectives and Success Criterium feed directly into your lesson's Learning Outcomes. Outcomes often aren't written down on the board, and are for us more than they are for the students, but should always be considered when planning a lesson. An Outcome is what you want your students to come away with, having met your clear and measurable Learning Objectives and Success Criterium. As I said before, 'Why are you teaching your lesson?', and what understanding, knowledge, or evidence of learning, are you expecting your students to leave with?

My advice is that you should always know why you are teaching a lesson, and you should plan your Learning Objective, and consider your Outcomes, before you start preparing the tangible aspects of your lesson (slides, worksheets, etc.). You need to know what and why you are teaching before you start building your lesson. Success Criteria can come into play after you've made, or while you're making, your resources. This isn't a hard and fast rule. Some teachers know exactly what they want their students to do to achieve their learning, prior to writing their first slide, but sometimes you will need to start building your lesson first to get a feel of what activities are appropriate, which will fit into the time constraints, and how exactly you want the learning to take place and be evidenced. It's like writing the introduction for an essay or dissertation, often you need to know what you've written before you can introduce it. Play around with this and see what best suits you, but by the time you are teaching your lesson, your students will want a clear and measurable LO, and SCs which specifically show them how they are expected to achieve their learning. I get my students to read out aloud the LO and SCs at the start of every lesson, and you may want to do this too. It's just another way of building structure and routine (more on these coming up), and gets everyone focused on the session's learning.

The Starter: Also referred to as 'bell work', as in work to be completed before the bell rings and the lesson-proper starts, the starter is your opportunity to quickly build a positive attitude to learning in your classroom, and to either recap on the previous lesson's learning, or introduce the current lesson's topic. In most instances, a starter shouldn't last longer than 5 minutes, to ensure it doesn't eat away too much time from the main tasks of your lesson, but this isn't a hard and fast rule. Use your initiative, there may be times when the current lesson can't begin until you are sure the topic of the previous lesson has been fully learnt, and more importantly, retained. This may call for a longer starter – remember, it's your classroom and this should be **your decision!**

Here are some examples of starter activities which can be used in your classroom:

- **Recap Questions:** 'What are the main push and pull factors leading to increased rates of rural to urban migration in Brazil?', 'What were the names of Henry VIII's wives? Can you write them down in the order in which he married them?', 'Can you rewrite the sentences on the board, adding possessive apostrophes in the correct places?'. An oldy, but a goody; simple recap questions of the previous lesson's learning are a great way to ensure your students are back focused on the current topic, and can build off of what they've previously learnt. Rosenshine (2012) opens his '*Principles of Instruction*' by reviewing previous learning, going into further detail on how recap can both strengthen learning and lead to fluent recall[18]. You may want to consider giving his work a read.

- **Challenge Grids:** A challenge grid is a twist on the classic recap question. Have prepared on the board a selection of questions, formatted into a grid. These can range from recap to pre-learning (learning which you are covering soon) questions. Colour-code the questions, with a key, to identify the questions in a range of difficulty e.g easier questions, or questions covered in the last lesson, in green, and harder questions in red, with middling questions in orange. Either allow the students to pick their own questions, and pick their own level of challenge, or assign each colour a number of points, 1 point for a green question, 3 for a red, for example, and challenge the students to accumulate a points total for a reward.

---

[18] Rosenshine, B. (2012) Principles of Instruction: Research-Based Strategies That All Teachers Should Know. *American Educator*. 39 (3), p 12-19

State two immediate responses to a tectonic hazard which could reduce the number of deaths	' Monitoring and predicting are the best ways to reduce the risk of tectonic hazards' Use evidence to challenge this statement	To what extent do the responses to a tectonic hazard vary between LICs and HICs
Outline two primary effects of volcanic eruption	' LICs always suffer when an earthquake hits' Use evidence to support this statement	Outline two secondary effects of an earthquake
Assess the social and environmental effects for a tectonic hazard you have studied	Explain how global atmospheric systems affect the weather and climate of the tropics	Compare the similarities and differences between a constructive and destructive plate boundary
Describe the global distribution of volcanoes	Explain why so many people live in tectonic hazardous areas	Explain how prediction might help to reduce the effects of a volcanic eruption
State two differences between continental and oceanic crust	Define the term ' Natural Hazard'	Explain how earthquakes are created at conservative plate boundaries

= 1 point = 2 points = 3 points

Figure 4- Challenge Grid Starter

- **Crosswords/Word Searches/Anagrams:** Any basic word exercises can be used to introduce key terms, or to remind students of terms from previous lessons. To expand on this, give your students dictionaries, and instruct them to find definitions for any new key words introduced.

- **The 5 Ws:** What? Why? Where? When? Who? And sometimes, the H, How? Either on the board, or even better, printed onto an A3 sheet per table, give your students access to an image related to the lesson's learning. Around the image, or in their books, the students must make educated guesses on what they're looking at, by answering the 5 Ws. This works best printed because they can write the W (and H) subheadings around the image, and then list what they can see/infer. A brilliant, visual, way of introducing a topic.

- **Match-up Activity:** Match key words to definitions or calculations to the correct answers. These can be recaps of terms/calculations learnt in the previous lessons, or pre-learning for the topic coming up.

- **Cross-curricular Exercises:** A common problem found in many schools is that they may have excellent departments, but that these departments can become isolated and not communicate well with each other. You are of course very passionate about your subject, but try not to forget that your students are studying many subjects and our job is to mould them into holistic well-balanced young people. With this in mind, try to incorporate cross-curricular exercises into your starters. Below is an example of a maths-based starter for a geography lesson. Maybe you could start a religion or a biology lesson with a poem writing activity, based on some prior learning? Or could you get your students up and roleplaying a scene studied in history or business? With a touch of imagination, the possibilities are endless.

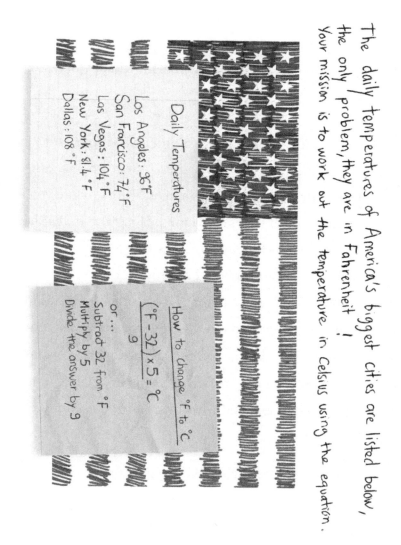

Figure 5- Cross-Curricular Starter

Usually, you, the teacher, should not be *teaching* during a starter. The starter should be on the board, or printed-out, ready for students to come in and attempt independently. This is your opportunity to welcome students into your classroom and to complete registers. Keep this in mind when developing your starters, you do not want to make starters that are too difficult and will not allow your students to get on with them without your support.

Introducing The Lesson's Main Topic: Soon you will have a well-oiled routine of welcoming students into your room, allowing them to independently attempt their starters and bell-work, while you take the register and complete any other necessary admin. Don't fret if this starter routine isn't perfect straight away. How long it takes for students to settle in a classroom will differ from school to school and from class to class, but just like when 'setting out your stall' and building your 'school reputation', you can train your students on what your expectations are when coming into your classroom. Make rewards and consequences (focusing on rewards) freely available during this training period. Remember – young minds **want** to know what is expected of them, and what they can and cannot get away with. You just need to make it clear.

Once this has been achieved, it is time to introduce your lesson's **main topic**. As a rule of thumb, I would recommend having **one** main topic per lesson. I also teach in the real world, and I know time is a commodity we as teachers rarely have enough of. One of the issues of wider teaching that you will come across is the difficulty of trying to fit an entire GCSE curriculum into only two (sometimes three) school years. Bearing in mind you may only see that GCSE class for one or two hours each week. Sometimes we do have to squeeze two (or three) topics into one lesson. But, in an ideal world, I'd advice one key idea per lesson. It's a balancing act. We need to teach everything on the syllabus, but can a 14, 15, or 16 year old mind really retain three topics worth of information, thrown at them at lightning speed, within the space of an hour? (Often a real world 45 minutes, when behaviours, admin, and AOB are tossed into the mix- misbehaving projectors anyone?[19] [20]). One thing actually *learnt* is superior to three or four things covered but not retained.

After the starter, and reading through of LO and SCs, the introduction of your main topic is when you should be first spending time *teaching* in your lesson. There are different ways of putting the key information across (see: **Teaching Methods**), and I would advise teaching in the way you feel is best suited to the students in your room, and to also mix it up from time to time. Students don't want to always listen to you drone on lecture style (not that we *drone on*, do we?), but similarly, you might have previously made a fantastic carousel activity which introduced key learning for the lesson's topic, but your students will not want to do this week-in-week-out. Utilise a variety of both tried-and-tested, and more imaginative methods, to get this initial information across. I was once given some valuable advice, which I will share

---

[19] Saloviita, T. (2013) Classroom Management and Loss of Time at the Lesson Start: A Preliminary Study. *European Journal of Educational Research*. 2 (4), p.167-170
[20] Shepherd, J. (2009) Pupil misbehaviour costs others a lesson a day. *The Guardian*. Available at: https://www.theguardian.com/education/2009/apr/14/pupil-misbehaviour-lesson-wasted

now with you: **Your trainee and ECT years** (Newly Qualified Teacher year, back in my day) **are there for you to make mistakes**. Be imaginative. As I've mentioned before, try new and different teaching styles and methods. You might find something that works brilliantly and suits your personal teaching style. Don't fear making mistakes, we learn from them and become better teachers because of our experiences.

Main Activity: During a lesson, your students should be working harder than you. Many new teachers make the mistake of thinking this is the opposite way around, and spend the hour presenting information, then dashing about, marking, teaching one-to-one, teaching smaller groups, the whole class, and ultimately, burning out. You are not there to do the work for your students. If you feel pressured to have 30 perfect workbooks from a class of students, with all the answers correct, triple-marked, and every last thing laid out and presented as neatly as humanly possible, **consider if this is a healthy school environment for you to be in**. That's not to say we shouldn't encourage neat work (I often say, if I can't read something, then neither can an examiner), but your students' workbooks are just that: workbooks. There should be mistakes in them, they should be a work in progress that tells a story of a student who is working and improving over time.

You are there to teach the lesson's topic, the lesson's *learning*. And your students are there to then display they have retained some of this learning, by completing set activities. They are the ones completing these activities, and they should be the ones working the hardest. Let's have a look at some methods, some key elements of pedagogy, used for introducing a lesson's main topic and activities.

Teaching Methods:

Teacher-centric: Teacher-centric teaching is your 'traditional' form of teaching. And, sometimes, things are traditional for a reason. It feels like there has been a push against teacher-centric teaching in recent years, but sometimes there is no substitute for a professional, with a strong subject knowledge, speaking and sharing that knowledge with their students. There are, though, methods to improve the learning potential of the teacher-centric method.

First step, and it may seem an obvious one, use visual aids. The idea that students have different 'learning styles', and that there are visual, auditory or kinetic learners has been widely debunked[21], and has been for years (yet, irritatingly, stills crops up regularly in schools). However, visuals alongside explanation, in the form of hand-drawn diagrams on white-boards or real-world example photographs within slideshow presentations, can be a beneficial tool in both making trickier-to-explain concepts easier to digest ('Oh, now I get it!'), and in retaining the engagement of a class ('See, *this* is

---

[21] Newton, P., and Salvi, A. (2020) How Common Is Belief in the Learning Styles Neuromyth, and Does It Matter? A Pragmatic Systematic Review. *Frontiers in Education.* Available at: https://www.frontiersin.org/articles/10.3389/feduc.2020.602451/full

what the aftermath of an earthquake can look like!')[22]. There has even been some exciting development in how music can be beneficial to learning in the classroom[23]. I'm by no-means an expert here, and if you are a music teacher you will already know more than me, but it's clear music is no longer just for the music rooms, and you may want to read Hallam's (2015) 'The Power of Music' report[24] to find out more.

Second step, and it's another one you're probably doing without thinking too much about it, is to ensure there's regular formative assessment, also known as Assessment for Learning, which can be achieved as easily as with some directed questioning (although there are many other options as well). We will cover the pros and cons of both formative and summative assessment later on (See: **Assessment**). Regular questioning of students, to check they have been listening and retained some of the learning, is a quick and powerful method of making sure both that your students are engaged, and that you are pitching the lesson at the right level to allow them to access their learning. I prefer directed questioning (you, the teacher, picking specific students to answer a question), rather than a 'hands up' approach, as with hands up you'll often find you'll get the same small group putting their hands up and answering your questions each time[25]. It has been found in some

---

[22] Gangwer, T. (2009) *Visual Impact, Visual Teaching: Using Images to Strengthen Learning*. 2nd edn. Corwin Press: Thousand Oaks, California.

[23] Caplin, M. and Childs, L., (2021) *Why you need to embed music into every lesson*. Available at: https://www.tes.com/magazine/teaching-learning/primary/why-you-need-embed-music-every-lesson

[24] Hallam, S. (2015) *The Power of Music*. Music Education Council: London.

[25] Glenmoor and Winton Academies. (2018) *What is "No Hands up? @ GW?"*. [PowerPoint presentation]. Available at:

studies that only 30% of a class will regularly put their hands up and try to answer questions[26], which may be due to disengagement, students not feeling comfortable taking the place of one of the regular contributors in the classroom, or anxiety linked to either getting the question wrong or not being picked to answer. Directed questioning means any student could be picked at any time. It shouldn't sound as ominous as that maybe does, but it should hopefully lead to more students paying attention and actively engaging, as they know they may be picked to recite a piece of the learning at any given moment. It also allows you, as the teacher, to get a much wider spread of the understanding in your classroom, and to even direct certain questions at specific students, if you wanted to double-check their understanding of an idea or topic. Some schools have their own policy on questioning, being for or against 'hands up', or having a targeted group with priority when it comes to answering questions (Pupil Premium First[27], is a common one), but unless directed otherwise, I would advise making sure all the students are picked to answer a question *at least* once every other lesson, if not once a lesson (depending on class sizes), and that you don't just pick on the students you think will know the answers. It's a balancing act, as anything in teaching is. You don't want to pick on a student who is trying hard but struggling, and may be embarrassed to give an incorrect answer, but it's also our job to make sure everyone is actively engaged in the learning, and to assess their

---

https://www.glenmoor.org.uk/Portals/2/No%20Hands%20up%20presentation.pdf?ver=2018-06-13-123859-243

[26] Larkey, S. (2015) *Reducing Anxiety and Increasing Participation with a NO HANDS UP Rule*. Available at: http://suelarkey.com.au/wp-content/uploads/2015/03/reduceanxiety.pdf

[27] HM Government. (2022) *Pupil premium*. Available at: https://www.gov.uk/government/publications/pupil-premium/pupil-premium

understanding. If a student is struggling, throw them an easier question, or something you've gone over with them one-to-one recently, this still shows learning has taken place, and can also boost confidence – and is that not also a huge part of our jobs? The Glenmoor and Winton Academies (2018) summarise the benefits of a 'No Hands Up' policy they've implemented in their classrooms, with benefits ranging from reduced panic in students, something that can particularly impact students on the autism spectrum, as well as any others, who fear not being picked and missing out[28], to improved levels of attention from students, and improved Assessment for Learning (AFL) opportunities, as the teacher can direct their questioning to specific students who may not have shown their understanding elsewhere. An overview of the benefits they've discovered can be found on the next page[29]:

---

[28] Larkey, S. (2015) *Reducing Anxiety and Increasing Participation with a NO HANDS UP Rule*. Available at: http://suelarkey.com.au/wp-content/uploads/2015/03/reduceanxiety.pdf

[29] Glenmoor and Winton Academies. (2018) *What is "No Hands up? @ GW?"*. [PowerPoint presentation]. Available at: https://www.glenmoor.org.uk/Portals/2/No%20Hands%20up%20presentation.pdf?ver=2018-06-13-123859-243

<u>Positive impacts of a 'No Hands Up' strategy</u>

- Allows the teacher to implement greater differentiation through targeted questioning
- Reduces panic in students
- Fosters a culture of managing impulsivity
- Improves attention levels
- Provides greater AFL (Assessment for Learning) opportunities
- Increases opportunity for all students to actively engage with their learning

Figure 6- Positive Impacts Of A 'No Hands Up' Strategy (Adapted from Glenmoor and Winton Academies, 2018)

Modelling: This is more of a sub-section of teacher-centric teaching than its own method, but it's vitally important and deserves its own subheading. Words are brilliant, but they can only get us so far (that's why we introduce images, sounds, and directed questioning), and as powerful as images can be in complimenting a point or idea, a teacher practically modelling a piece of work will often engage, and stick with a student, even more.

You can model anything. And you should be able to. If you are not confident in what you are teaching, you will struggle to teach it. That's not to say we should know everything- but before teaching a specific lesson you may need to brush up on your knowledge of long division, or the dramatic methods of Stanislavsky, or the themes behind Dicken's work, or whatever you are teaching, because you need to be confident in your subject knowledge, before you teach it. And a good measure of subject knowledge strength is whether or not you can model it.

I like to model on the whiteboard, old-school manual modelling. I've spent countless hours drawing diagrams showing a river's meander turning into an oxbow lake over time, or how the greenhouse gases that circulate our planet trap in the sun's rays, and it's also fairly straightforward to model mathematical equations and how to work them out. Some modelling, such as longer essay-style questions, or the annotating of English texts, is harder to draw up on the whiteboard. For these, you may want to complete the task on paper, using different colours to show your method, and have this photocopied and ready to hand out around the class. Some modelling can also be done on your powerpoint slides, although this is less tangible and we must be careful that we are still modelling, and not merely teaching through our slides. Try modelling practically in advance, taking photographs, and incorporating these into your slides – this works well in practical lessons such as Design Technology or Cooking, where you may have made something in advance which can't be modelled in real-time, such as the baking of a cake.

The final, and arguably best, option, is to use an overhead projector. These were once commonly found in schools up and down the country, and are now making a bit of a resurgence – but your ability to use one will ultimately come down to access and whether you can request an OHP as part of your school budget. If you can, these are ideal tools to model work in real-time, showing your students exactly what is expected. It also offers them the proof, and confidence, that the task is both possible and *manageable*. If you can work it out, in real-time, in front of them, then so can they. Sometimes, the old ways really are the best ways.

Student-centric: It should be no surprise that all lessons must have an element (and usually a majority element) of student-centric learning; learning where the emphasis is on the students discovering a large part of the learning for themselves through research and activities, and learning in practical and proactive ways. Schools are not university lecture halls, and many students will switch off if they think they're expected to sit and listen and make notes for a solid hour from a teacher-centric session[30].

So, how can we best engage our students and make sure the golden rule is being followed: That they are working (and therefore *learning*) harder than we are?

Worksheets and Textbooks: The most common form of student-centric learning and assessing is to introduce and teach a topic/idea, and then have the students complete an activity to show they have retained and learnt some (all?) of the presented information. These activities will often take the form of worksheets, or questions and activities from textbooks. For example, let's say I've just taught a year 8 geography class about the Push and Pull Factors

---

[30] Brain Balance. (2022) *Normal Attention Span Expectations By Age.* Available at: https://www.brainbalancecenters.com/blog/normal-attention-span-expectations-by-age#:~:text=Childhood%20development%20experts%20generally%20say,focus%20on%20a%20given%20task.

leading to rural-to-urban migration in Brazil. I will now want them to complete a worksheet, highlighting factors as either 'Push' or 'Pull', while also utilizing their ability to make a key, and then write a short paragraph answering the question, 'Why is there an increase in the rates of Brazilians migrating from The Caatinga to Rio de Janeiro?'. The paragraph question itself may have come directly out of the pages of a Geography textbook.

The electricity regularly doesn't work in your village, and you have no access to a computer.	Your older brother moved to Brasilia last year, found a job, and sends money back home each month.
Poor think soils in The Caatinga makes farming extremely difficult.	There are big hospitals with lots of medicine available in Brasilia.
There are no schools in your village.	Brasilia is Brazil's capital city. It is wealthy and there are lots of rich people living there.
The weather in the rural north is hot and dry, making if very difficult to grow crops.	There are lots of schools, colleges and universities in Brasilia.
There are a range of jobs available in Brasilia, all of which pay higher wages than those in The Caatinga.	The only jobs available in the rural north are in farming.

Figure 7- Categorising Activity Focusing On Push and Pull Factors Leading To Migration Within Brazil

If they can do this, I can confidently say they are working towards meeting their Learning Objective, which could be: *To understand the factors causing rural to urban migration within Brazil, and to be able to categorise these as either Push or Pull Factors.*

Some people in and around schools may try to tell you that using textbooks is a bad thing. That it's lazy. That it isn't engaging enough for your students. **This is total nonsense**. As with all methods of teaching, I wouldn't recommend teaching from a textbook every lesson, as the repetition very well may become dull for your students, and while you are utilizing textbooks, I also wouldn't recommend just handing them out and asking your students to, 'Read through pages 67 – 70 and complete the tasks' (Ah, old-school substitute teacher lessons. We've all been there). But using textbooks as a resource for assessing learning, after some high-quality teacher-centric teaching? Brilliant. That's what they're there for! Not only are most high-quality textbooks chocka-full of fantastic questions with which to assess your student's learning, they've also got colour images, worked examples, and relevant information, which can all aid the learning process. When used proactively, textbooks can be amazing resources. You are going to assess the learning with questions anyway, so whether these questions come from the whiteboard, a worksheet, or a textbook, doesn't particularly make a difference (but try to change regularly between the three to keep things fresh!).

Carousel Activities: I mentioned this earlier on, so I'd better explain what I was talking about. I love a carousel activity. They take a little bit of prep-work to organise, but the payoff is always worth it.

For a carousel activity to take place, you must arrange resources around the room prior to the students turning up. These can be fact-files, images, tactile objects, or activities for the students to complete. As the students come into the room, set them into small groups (approx. groups of 3

– 4, depending on class size). Each group should be directed to one of the resources around the room, and then at regular intervals, you will direct each group to move to their next resources (e.g. 'Everyone move one resource to the right').

I was first introduced to carousel activities while observing a geography lesson focusing on the layers of the rainforest. Around the room were fact-files, sticky tacked to the wall, providing information on the four different rainforest layers, the *forest floor, understory, canopy,* and *emergent layer.* The groups were tasked to go around with their own information-gathering sheets, research the different layers, and then towards the end of the lesson, answer an essay-style question comparing them. These lessons get the students out of their seats and get them working with independence and proactiveness, as they go around the room finding the answers/completing tasks themselves, as opposed to listening directly to a teacher-centric session followed by completing the same task at the same time as everyone else. In my experience students respond really positively to these lessons, and I encourage you to try them out.

Menu Activities: This is another activity which takes a bit of preparation. Remember to go into these with a level of realism, not **every** lesson needs to be 'outstanding', and not every lesson should be taking you an hour-plus to create. However, you do owe it to your students to provide consistently high levels of teaching (which comes in many forms), and sometimes the graft will need putting in. The bad news? This is unfairly balanced so that your hours will be longer planning and creating at the start of your teaching career (remember that 35% drop-out rate?), but the good news is that once you have created a high-quality resource or lesson, it can be used again and again for years to come (until the government decides to entirely rejig the curriculum, but that's another story for another time).

Menu activities take a bit of extra preparation, but then on the flipside, shouldn't be too cumbersome when it comes to actually teaching the lesson. Students will come into your room to find a menu of activities on the board, or printed out for them individually. These should be set out like food menus, with a choice of three starters, three mains, and three dessert options. The students will need to complete (as a minimum) one starter, one main and one dessert task. Of the tasks, the first task in each section is the most scaffolded and aimed towards your students who need added support, the middle task is, you guessed it, somewhere in the middle, and the third task is aimed towards your higher ability learners. Make these menus fun! I like to add a 'spicy rating' to my mains and give the tasks food-related names. In my example, my lower ability task is a Chicken Korma, with a rating of one chilli pepper, followed by a two chilli pepper Lamb Balti, and a three chilli pepper King Prawn Vindaloo for my highest ability learners and those who want to push themselves further. This example focuses on tornados and the 2005 Birmingham tornado case study, but this type of activity can be implemented for any subject or topic.

The increased preparation here comes from you initially creating nine different tasks. The starters, in the above example, wouldn't take too long to plan. They are simple question and answer starters, based on work covered in the previous lessons, and the differentiation (more on this coming) can also be shown via outcomes, as well as by which question is picked. 'What is the Fujita Scale?' may be a one-sentence answer (it's a scale of tornado intensity, based on the damage a tornado inflicts – I'll award myself a gold star), while the third question, 'How much damage was caused by the Birmingham tornado?', when properly answered, could be a mini-essay. A higher-level student would break their answer down into Economic, Social and Environmental damages, sandwiched between a mini-introduction and conclusion. A student who needs more support very well may also have a go at this question, but may not break it down into the three different areas of damage, and therefore you can tailor their support accordingly.

Students having a go and pushing themselves to answer potentially harder questions is another key benefit of the Menu activity. Perhaps a student has answered the three easier tasks and comes to you saying they have finished their work. With no extra thinking or planning required, you can direct them to another task on the board (one you feel will push them, but which will still be achievable), again, differentiating and extending that student's learning. Even a student who has completed the three harder tasks, will still then have the middle tasks to work on.

Preparing your three main and dessert tasks may take a little more preparation, but I guarantee your students will love it. Every now and again, I fully recommend a Menu activity lesson. Yum!

Time for a CURRY

Pick up your starter, main and dessert

1. STARTER

PAPADUMS

What is the Fujita scale?

ONION BHAJI

Why should you stay away from windows during a tornado?

TIKKA PRAWNS

How much damage was caused by the Birmingham tornado?

2. MAIN

CHICKEN KORMA

Explain how we could reduce the risks from a tornado

LAMB BALTI

Create a mind-map showing how the tornado formed and what damage it caused in Birmingham

KING PRAWN VINDALOO

The damage caused by the Birmingham tornado was greater than that caused by tornados in the Midwestern USA' answer using PEE paragraphs

3. DESSERT

VANILLA ICE-CREAM

Peer assess your partner's work

MANGO LASSI

Peers assess your partner's SPAG (Spelling, Grammar, and Punctuation)

GULAB JAMUN

Describe the formation of a tornado

Figure 8- Menu Activity

Discussions, Debates and Role-play: Not everything learnt needs to be written down. Evidencing learning and progression has increased considerably in schools over the last decade, with a recent National Education Union (2018) survey finding that pressures to increase student scores/grades, and evidencing such, was the most frequent workload driver cited by teachers[31]. And a certain level of evidencing in schools is both necessary and important, you need to have a record of how your students are doing so that you can plan for them, push them academically, and assess them accordingly, and parents/carers also like to see a record of how their child is performing and progressing. However, there is still a place in modern education for learning which isn't necessarily written down and recorded, where you have witnessed your students *showing* you what they've learnt. Here lies class discussions, debates, and role-play.

I once taught an English module on the legend of Robin Hood, looking at the story's origin, how it's presented through different mediums, and then questioning what it meant to be good, bad, and a criminal. This last part presented a perfect opportunity to work in some debate and role-play. We created a courtroom scene in the classroom, with a Robin Hood and his lawyer arguing for Robin's innocence and why he was a good guy, a Sheriff of Nottingham and his lawyer, arguing that Robin was a criminal who needed locking up, a judge to hear the arguments (and play referee), and finally, the rest of the class was placed on a jury, listening to the arguments and then debating amongst themselves whether or not they felt Robin had committed

---

[31] National Education Union. (2018) *Teachers and Workload*. Available at: https://neu.org.uk/media/3136/view

a crime, was inherently good or bad (or that ever-present grey area of 'both'), and whether he should be sent to jail.

Role-plays and debates can be used for almost any subject. Different teams debating who should have been the rightful king of England in the run-up to the battle of Hastings. Role-plays on the pressures and dangers of smoking or trying drugs. Debating whether the UK government should invest more in renewable energy technologies? Role-play the discovery of famous scientific or mathematical findings. Whatever the subject matter, the key to a high-quality debate or role-play is that the students get ample time before the activity to research their roles and arguments, and it can also be beneficial for you to pick your students 'sides' during a debate or discussion, so that they are not only arguing for things they already agree with. It is important for students to understand other peoples' perspectives and ideas, and to fully research and present these, even if they personally disagree with them. Back in my example, I had students arguing for Robin Hood to be locked away for the rest of his life, stating that a crime is a crime regardless of the reasoning behind it, even when they saw him as a flawed hero who was trying to protect the poor people of Nottingham. These debates can always be followed up with a written task, where the students *can* present their own perspectives and ideas, so that this itch is ultimately scratched.

This is in no way an exhaustive list of student-centric learning activities. You could make quizzes, create detective scenarios where students follow clues towards their learning outcomes, you could write essay-style answers for your students to go over and mark, looking for examples of good and poor practice.

The list is endless. Hopefully, I have given you enough examples to get the ball rolling, but my advice would be to be creative! Young (and older) people learn in a variety of different ways, and through a bit of trial of error you will soon work out what works best for your students.

The Plenary: Plenaries are short tasks (usually no-more than 5 minutes in length) that review and consolidate the lesson's learning. They're a good opportunity to check whether the Learning Objective has been met, and to assess, in a quick and informal way, just how much *learning* your students are leaving your classroom having gained.

I would recommend trying to work a plenary into all of your lessons where possible, with rare exceptions such as when students are coming in and continuing to complete coursework which may take them multiple sessions. Any lesson where *any* new learning has taken place (which should be pretty much every lesson), can be reviewed. This includes lessons where the learning and lesson objectives span multiple sessions – some learning has surely taken place in each session, and that can be reviewed and consolidated.

Here are some examples of plenary activities which can be used in your classroom:

Review Questions: Sometimes the simplest options are also the most effective. If you want to review a lesson's learning, ask your students questions on the topic that's been covered. This could be as easy as asking informal directed questions to students of your selecting at the end of a session. This is a quick and simple method of getting a rough consensus on what's been learnt in the room, although unless you have the time to ask each individual student, you won't get a full overview of each student's learning (and sometimes, that's fine!). Alternatively, you could take a more formal approach, with questions written on the board to be copied into books and answered. Consider RAGing these questions (Red, Amber, Green, with varying levels of difficulty), and either allowing your students to pick the questions best suited to them, or insisting that your students answer the easier questions first and work their way up to the harder options.

Use your teacher judgment to determine when review questions are best suited. If you've just taught a question/answer heavy lesson, possibly working through worksheets or textbooks, students may be weary to answer more questions at the end of the session. Alternatively, if you've had a debate or role-play heavy lesson, where lots has been learnt but not necessarily written down, utilising written down review questions can be a great way of evidencing that learning.

5 Things Handprint: A plenary probably more commonly seen in primary schools, but which I guarantee big kids will enjoy as well. Have your students draw an outline of their handprint in their books, and in each finger, and the thumb, write one thing they've learnt in the lesson. This plenary takes absolutely no prior planning from you, yet is a great, and simple, method, of getting your students to think about, and therefore start to cement in their minds, what they've learnt during the lesson.

Transform: This plenary is a little more abstract, but can also be hugely beneficial for a certain type of student; the arty type, or the type who struggles with or is resistant to lots of writing. However, any student may enjoy and get something out of this.

Ask your students to transform either the lesson's learning (as a concept), or a particular aspect you have selected (such as an extract of text), into an image. For some, this may seem an easy task, for others, a little tricker, but be assured, as long as the student is fully engaged with this task (and not jotting down a quick, unidentifiable, scribble), they are testing their cognition, making connections between the academic and artistic elements of their brain, and are doing so much more than merely drawing a picture. It takes a great deal of contemplation to take a concept or a stimulus and consider how that can be transformed into an image. The golden rule? Absolutely no words allowed.

Summarise: Again, select either the whole lesson's learning or a particular element, and ask your students to summarise it in a number of words of your choosing e.g. 'Explain what photosynthesis is in only ten words.'

Differentiation

No two students are the same. Some of your students will have SEND (Special Educational Needs or Disabilities[32]), some will be EAL (English as an Additional Language – speaking a mother tongue which is something other than English[33]), some may be PP (Pupil Premium - disadvantaged students who meet certain criteria, such as coming from a low-income household or being a carer or in care themselves[34]), and even those who fit none of these, or any other defined categories, will be individual, and will have their own skillsets, their own personalities, and their own challenges. How can we then, as teachers, provide high-quality education for a full class of unique and individual students?

The answer, is differentiation; having different, or edited, activities within a lesson for students of different needs. Am I saying you need to provide thirty different tasks, per lesson, for thirty different students? **Absolutely not**. But you will need to be mindful of your Higher, Middle and Lower Ability workers, and any other students whose needs require a differentiated task.

---

[32] HM Government. (2022) *Children with special educational needs and disabilities (SEND).* Available at: https://www.gov.uk/children-with-special-educational-needs
[33] HM Government. (2022) *English proficiency: pupils with English as additional language.* Available at: https://www.gov.uk/government/publications/english-proficiency-pupils-with-english-as-additional-language
[34] HM Government. (2022) *Pupil premium.* Available at: https://www.gov.uk/government/publications/pupil-premium/pupil-premium

Let me give you an example. I taught a class with a girl who had Scotopic Sensitivity Syndrome. This is a syndrome (and I'm no doctor here) which affects a person's sensitivity to light and colour. What it effectively meant in my classroom, was that this girl couldn't read black text off white paper well and so needed all her worksheets printed out on pink paper. That's all that was needed, and it was a quick change I needed to make at the printer before lessons, to ensure she could properly access all of her worksheets. That is an example of differentiation to ensure this student could fully access her resources and take part in her learning.

Other times, differentiation will be a *little* more complex. I will be honest with you here, I know early on in your career you will be swamped with planning, teaching, marking, and all the other (often nonsense) admin, such as forming target grades, preparing for parents' evenings, staff meetings ('This surely could have been an email'), and everything else teachers are expected to do, so no, I won't tell you that you're expected to differentiate for each individual student, in all your lessons, and effectively plan three (four, five?) lessons for every one. What I will say is that you need to decide early on who your Higher, Middle and Lower Ability learners are in your classes, and you will **often** (but not always), have to prepare higher and lower-ability activities/worksheets ready for them. I would especially recommend having these prepared and ready for any observation lessons you've got coming up (See: **Observations**). This normally means finding or creating your first worksheet, I tend to make higher ones first and differentiate them down, but this is just a personal choice, and then editing it into higher/lower ability versions. Take out questions which will be plainly inaccessible, and potentially daunting and confidence-knocking, for certain students. Turn a question that requires a PEE (Point, Evidence, Explanation) paragraph answer, into an answer which can be written as bullet points. Don't always differentiate the same way, as when creating activities, but in a situation where you have a student who cannot write long paragraphs, bullet points are a way of determining the *understanding* rather than the ability of the student's written English. Another time, it may be that certain student needs images alongside a writing frame to support their attempt at longer-form writing.

You can also differentiate with support. If you are lucky to have TAs (Teaching Assistants) in your room, make sure they are focusing on the students who require extra support and are guiding them through their learning. If you are going to attempt essay-based questions, have sentence starters available on the board which some students can refer to and use to help them get started. Another easy win is to differentiate with your seating plan. Make sure any students who need extra support are in your front row, or at the end of rows, so that it's easier for you to physically get to them and support them. You will likely be asked how you are differentiating to support your classes, and this is an easy one to implement and bring up.

A lot of the lesson activities I've been through have differentiation built into them (i.e., The Menu Activity), and I will say just one more thing on the subject. When I differentiate, I like to ensure all the students are doing the same task, with the same Learning Objectives and Outcomes, but with different levels of support and differently edited worksheets/activities. Some teachers have in the past excluded students from activities with lots of reading if they think they struggle to read, and instead had them, say, read a CVC (single syllable three-letter words) book, or colour, during this time. How then is that student expected to improve their reading, if they're not being involved and being allowed to have a go? In this situation, I wouldn't want to embarrass or stress-out the student by asking them to read aloud a text which is above their reading age, but I would expect the student to use a ruler or their finger to follow the text while others read. Or, if possible, I would find or create a simplified text presenting largely the same information, specifically for them. I would largely recommend having all of your students engage in the same learning, with different levels of support. As with all the advice in this book, this is an opinion and there will be exceptions. If your school offers fantastic intervention sessions, where a TA or another teacher can take out students to do a structured session on reading or maths skills, which you believe would benefit them more in the long run than being in the lesson you're currently teaching, then take this opportunity. But while they are in your classroom, most students will have the ability to engage in any lesson's learning, when the right support is put in place.

What's The Plan?

Now you've had an overview of how a lesson can be structured, and some example activities you can use, you're probably wondering, 'How should I use this information to actually *plan* my lesson?' (or, alternatively, 'What is this guy on about, and is it too late to get a refund for this book?').

As I mentioned when I opened this section, what's expected of your planning will largely be dependent on your own school's policy. However, there are some aspects you are likely to need to consider, whether or not they are explicitly part of any whole-school policy. These are things like your timing, and the appropriateness of your tasks (you will quickly find a lesson can start to go off the rails if a task is so easy a class completes it in no time, or so hard that they can't really access it and ever begin). There is one fact which is true of all teachers' planning, as with the creating of activities, planning will need to be more in-depth, and therefore will take you longer, at the start of your career than when you are a more experienced teacher. There are a few reasons for this:

1. You may initially be brushing up on your subject knowledge, and in a sense, teaching yourself lesson content before you teach it to your students – this will become much less of an issue as time passes, and you become increasingly familiar with your curriculum.

2. Early on in your career, you will need time to consider which activities work best with which lessons. You may think to yourself, 'Would review questions or a summarising activity be the better plenary option to review this particular lesson's learning?' Later on, knowing what activity to place where will become second nature.

3. You will need to create more detailed plans early on, as you will be less confident and less sure (probably) how a high-quality lesson runs (and that's OK!). There is no shame in having a plan at hand to refer to as you teach, in fact it's something I highly recommend. This will be hugely beneficial in helping you keep to your timings. Do not fear though, as you grow in experience, you will become much more

knowledgeable about how your lessons should run and what the timings of your activities should be. Your planning may move from detailed planning sheets, to your own slides and resources, and a knowledge of how best to use them. Most experienced teachers follow long and medium-term plans, but **do not** need to write physical lesson plans for each individual lesson, a knowledge of their own lessons, resources, and most importantly, students, is enough – but you will need these plans to begin with.

The lesson plan templates on the following pages were provided to me by The University of Birmingham[35] when I went through my initial teacher training, and (I hope) they won't mind me sharing it with you. These are templates for **detailed** planning sheets, the kind I would recommend using during your training and ECT years. I also like to bust these out during a lesson observation (more on these coming up).

---

[35] University of Birmingham (2018) *Lesson Plan Template*. University of Birmingham. Unpublished

Usual Class Teacher:	Class:	Time:	Date:
Lesson Topic/Title:			
Relevance	Cross Curricular Links *(How does the lesson develop Literacy and Numeracy? SMSC? PSHE?)*		
Learning Objective(s)	Activities		Learning Outcome(s) *(How will I know that pupils have learned?)*
Resources	Other Adults *(How will you use a TA? How might you direct the usual class teacher as a TA?)*	Risk Assessment	N/A

Figure 9- Example Lesson Plan, Page 1 (University of Birmingham, 2018)

Time	Teacher Activity	Pupil Activity	Why?	Assessment Opportunities
2 minutes	Welcome students into room	Students to be selected to hand out books	Independence and SMSC – helping others	
11 minutes	Play short sci-fi film 'Final Offer'	Students to watch 'Final Offer'	This will give the students an example of a high-level sci-fi conversation	Directed questioning – what were the characters talking about?
2 minutes	Introduce LOs and Success Criteria	Students to copy this down into their books		
5 minutes	Discuss the Doctor Who and Darth Vader conversation	Students to read parts of the story aloud		Directed questioning – what might Doctor Who and Darth Vader be talking about?
15 minutes		Students to work through 'Sci-Fi character' worksheet in pairs, creating a profile on their partner's sci-fi character	Introduce the idea of building a 'character profile', which will be continued in their next lesson Team-working	
15 minutes	Introduce next task – students to write their own sci-fi conversations, using the example on the board to help them	Students to engage in creating their own sci-fi conversations	To assess whether learnt skills (inverted commas) can be used in practice	Staff to check whether inverted commas (speech marks) are being used correctly To check for Sci-Fi tropes within the conversations

Figure 10- Example Lesson Plan, Page 2 (University of Birmingham, 2018)

The planning template is broken down into two main sections. The first page is designed to get you thinking about the broader purpose of your lesson. Why is it **relevant**? We shouldn't just be teaching things for the sake of teaching things. Does your lesson content link back to prior learning, or wider life skills? Can you incorporate any **cross-curricular links**? It's vital our students' schooling is holistic, and just because we're teaching a science, or anything else, that doesn't mean we forget about the maths and English skills which can be incorporated into almost every lesson. When I was training, there was also a push for all lessons to incorporate an aspect of PSHE (Personal, Social and Health Education) and SMSC (Spiritual, Moral, Social and Cultural Development), in an effort to ensure we are teaching and moulding our young people into well-rounded global citizens – and so this should also be considered. Finding SMSC in a Religious Education lesson, an English lesson studying Dickens's 'A Christmas Carol', or in a Geography or History lesson focusing on a societal change, may come easily. It *might* be harder to find in a maths or physics lesson, but try to work it in as best you can, even if this only comes down to being firmer in encouraging good manners in your classroom. Moral growth, in my opinion, is just as important as academic.

The most important sections of this planning template, in my opinion, are for **Learning Objectives** and **Learning Outcomes**. It is vital your Learning Objectives, those clear and measurable objectives, link to your Learning Outcomes, what it is you want your students to have come away from of your lesson with. Together, these really should be the building blocks of your entire lesson, with any planned activities put in place to help our students reach those desired Learning Outcomes.

The second section is your timings. Here you break your lesson down into what you should be doing, what your students should be doing, the why, the assessment opportunities within the lesson, and, of course, how long each of these elements should take. Take a look at my included example for a breakdown of how this can be laid out. Mine are the timings for the first 50 minutes for an English lesson focusing on writing Sci-Fi style conversations. When planning timings, it's important to remember that **things will change, and things will go wrong**. From students acting up, to the age-old problem of the IT refusing to work, your timings may not always go to plan, **and that is OK** (I feel like I've said that a few times now, but it's true!**)**. It is also a truth that most new teachers think (and fear) they will run out of activities. The idea of (gasp) improvising with a group of rowdy teenaged students, can indeed be a terrifying one for an inexperienced teacher, and it is only natural a trainee teacher may over-plan in an attempt to avoid this situation. However, what then *tends* to happen, is that new teachers will try to cram too much into their lessons, will end up having to rush through activities that students often could benefit from spending some extended time on, and then (and everyone does this) run out of time for a plenary. If there was an archive somewhere of all the planned plenaries which never got to see the light of day in the classroom from trainee teachers and ECTs, it would be massive. And plenaries are vitally important, as we've discussed they're a key element for reviewing how much learning has taken place, they often guide us on what needs planning for and teaching in the upcoming lessons, and they establish an end-of-lesson routine which can put our students in the right frame of mind for leaving our classroom and transitioning to their next lesson or break. Every new teacher will miss out or rush through some, don't beat yourself up about that, but try your best early on to plan your timings accurately enough that you give yourself a healthy 5 minutes for a plenary at the end. It's a great habit to get in to.

I See You (Observations)

Now you're a cool, calm, collected teaching machine, who has planned and perfected their craft in the classroom. Ok, scratch that – no teacher's that. You're a competent and passionate new teacher, who's confident in the work you're doing. Maybe even still a little scared and feeling in-over-your-head, but doing the best you can. You may even have gone through an interview and been offered a fulltime teaching position in a school. Will they now leave you alone to get on with your job? Of course they won't! This is the bureaucratic world of teaching, after all.

As a trainee teacher, you can expect to be observed for every activity and lesson you teach. You're learning your trade, and the feedback an experienced teacher can give you is invaluable. As an ECT, there is no definitive stipulation around the timing or frequency of observations, only that it should happen at regular intervals[36], and the amount you are observed will therefore vary from school to school. In my personal experience though, ECTs are likely to be officially observed at least six times a year, once per half-term. This again can be a useful exercise as you craft and perfect(ish) your skills, given that the feedback you receive is beneficial, praising you for all you do well, while constructively advising you on things that can be improved (quality teachers teach teachers, as well as young people – the learning journey never ends!).

Where things get a little more questionable, are the annual observations which take place throughout the rest of your career as a qualified teacher. Schools shouldn't officially observe a teacher for more than three lessons per academic year, totalling a time of no-more than three hours[37], and in my experience many schools will only officially observe teachers twice an academic year, but may pop into lessons on a much more frequent basis. Whether or not this is a problem all depends on the school, and who is, and how frequently they are, popping in. A classroom door should always be open, and it is the job of the Head and Senior Leadership to know what is happening in their classrooms and to ensure the teaching within their schools is up to the expected standard. You will be a quality teacher, and as such, you'll have nothing to hide in your classroom. However, there is a flip side to this. Qualified teachers should feel trusted and respected enough to get on

---

[36] Department of Education. (2021) *Induction for early career teachers (England).* Department of Education: London
[37] National Education Union. (2020) *Guidance on classroom observation protocol in England.* Available at: https://neu.org.uk/advice/guidance-classroom-observation-protocol-england

with their job, and should never feel unfairly watched, or even harassed, while trying to teach. No one likes to be micromanaged, and in any respectable office environment (where most people spend their working days), you wouldn't expect an employer to be standing over your shoulder watching you type away, and you would likely question any undue micromanaging- and this shouldn't be any different in a school environment. In this sense, it's all about balance.

During an official observation, you should expect someone senior, usually a line-manager or member of SLT to watch either a whole, or a portion of your lesson. They should give you at least five working days' notice of when they intend to observe you[38], and preferably it would be good if they have spoken to you in advance about any particular aspects of your teaching they are looking to see. **Observations can be stressful**. Don't feel you're alone if you're not looking forward to an upcoming observation; I've been teaching for years, I dare say I have confidence in what I can deliver in my classroom, but I still get nervous when an observation comes up. It's natural to not perform at your best when you're being watched, and it's natural to get butterflies in your stomach before an observation. But try to remember, in a good school an observation should be a supportive process which helps to maintain school standards and improve your teaching. Even when you've been in the profession for twenty years, teaching evolves and we as teachers can always learn new things and better our output.

[38] National Education Union. (2020) *Guidance on classroom observation protocol in England*. Available at: https://neu.org.uk/advice/guidance-classroom-observation-protocol-england

But what can you do to ensure your observation goes well?

- **Prepare:** You're probably thinking, 'Well…duh', but preparation is arguably more important during an observation than at any other time (and arguably it definitely **should not be**, because we should be observed on how we actually teach, in the real-world, and not in a one-off 'super lesson'). Have a lesson plan printed and ready to hand. Have a pack of resources ready for your observer, so that they can easily follow your plan and see what each student is expected to be working through. This is particularly important in case something *does* go wrong! Your observer can see how your lesson was planned to progress and what the students would have gone on to achieve.

- **Have a Backup for Malfunctioning Technology:** You're planned, prepared, and ready to go…and the projector isn't working. These things happen, and sometimes it feels like they *especially* happen at all the wrong times (like just as an observer walks in). Have paper copies of resources ready, even if they're only a back-up. Even if nothing goes wrong, it shows you've considered the possibility and prepared so that no learning time is lost.

- **Warn Your Students:** How students will react to another adult in the room will depend on your class, but I advise pre-warning them. I will usually say, either at the end of the previous lesson, or at the beginning of the observation lesson, that, 'Sir/Miss will be joining us for this lesson, but it's nothing to worry about. They're watching me rather than watching you.' This can take the pressure off your students, and hopefully ensure the lesson runs as normally as possible.

- **Have Clear Differentiation:** Differentiation is something observers will be looking for. Have it clearly marked on your lesson plan/seating plan. Show your observer that you know your students and that you know how to ensure every student has the opportunity to meet their learning potential.

- **Don't Rush:** As when we're training to teach, even seasoned teachers can fall into the trap of rushing during an observation. Your mind's saying, 'SHOW THEM ALL THE AMAZING THINGS WE DO', and you don't want to be caught looking like you're not doing anything, so it's natural to want to rush through activities and rush around the room 'helping' students. Remember that students need time to access and complete tasks, and while it is important to be mobile in your classroom, it's more important that you're working with and supporting small groups through an activity, rather than doing laps and ticking and flicking. Be confident in your ability and in your lesson, and try your best to calm yourself down and deliver your regular quality teaching.

- **Show Off:** As I alluded to before, in a perfect world an observation should be a totally normal lesson and shouldn't require any special preparation. Afterall, they *should* want to get an idea of how your classroom normally runs. However, in the real world of teaching, observations often carry a certain level of expectation (hence the nerves and the added stress). Rather than letting this frighten you, use it as an opportunity to really show off! Add in a practical element, whether that's a science experiment, or a low-prep role-play activity. Put in place your rewards and consequences, ranging from verbal feedback to stickers for a 'Star of the Week' chart. Don't be afraid to say, 'I am a brilliant teacher, and I'm about to show you why!'.

- **Expect the Unexpected (and the expected):** We've spoken about projectors not working, but what about a fire drill? Or a student bursting into tears because of something that happened at home that morning? You can't prepare for every eventuality, but make sure you know school procedure for drills/emergencies, and consider your students and how they may react to others and unexpected situations. Could the very nature of an observation, and another adult in the room, trigger something in one of your students? Sometimes these *can* be expected. If you have particular behaviour issues with a member of your class, prepare for the worst and be confident in the procedures (warnings, parking, whether they need a soft touch or a firm word) in place to deal with this. If you have a student who needs short breaks during the lesson because they become overwhelmed by the classroom environment, have a '5-minute timeout' card printed and ready to use, and explain how it might be used within your lesson plan. You cannot prepare for everything, and if things do go wrong (and they might), you will need to deal with the ongoing situation as best you can. But if you can prepare and save yourself a headache later on – do it!

- **You've Got This:** Be confident in your own ability. Plan ahead, and don't allow yourself to become distressed if things do go wrong. We work in schools, we work with young people, and they are unpredictable! But you've got this! Discuss with your mentor, or another trusted colleague or family member, what you're planning to teach, and then go out there and do the best you can. That's all that can be asked of any of us. And if things don't go as smoothly as they possibly could have done, take onboard any feedback from your observer, keep doing what you do every day (changing lives – remember?), and come back stronger next time. An observation is just an opportunity to learn, and an opportunity to shine!

Marking

Have you ever heard a teacher say something along the lines of, 'I love teaching, but I hate all the marking'? Some will even go as far as to say it's the worst part of the job and one of the main things that impacts their work-life balance and leads to the job becoming unmanageable[39]. The last thing you want to do is complete your teacher training, find that you love being in the classroom, but end up one of these teachers who feels overwhelmed by their marking, and put off the job (we're back to that 35% drop-out rate again, aren't we?). So how do we make sure this doesn't become the case?

First of all, it's important to consider *why* we're marking. Feedback has been observed to be one of the biggest drivers in improving student attainment[40]. Teaching is all well and good, but if students come away from a lesson with a misconception or having frequently made the same mistake, and they will do this from time to time, learning is after all a journey, then

---

[39] National Education Union. (2018) *Teachers and Workload*. Available at: https://neu.org.uk/media/3136/view

[40] Hattie, J. (2009). *Visible Learning: A Synthesis of 800+ Meta-Analyses on Achievement*. London: Routledge.

feedback is a teacher's main tool is correcting these mistakes and improving their students' understanding. This feedback can come in a multitude of differing forms, from verbal feedback, to assessment, and also includes book marking.

Book marking then, can be hugely important. It's where we can go over our students' learning and look for common mistakes and misunderstandings, and while verbal feedback is brilliant (and highly recommended[41]), it can be quickly forgotten, whereas a written piece of feedback can be reread, discussed again at later dates, and used to show, in black and white (or red, or green), why mistakes were made and how they can be corrected and avoided next time. But this marked feedback is only any good when it is **meaningful**. 'Ticking and flicking', the act of flicking through the pages of a workbook to tick pieces of work absentmindedly, often done to meet some whole-school marking policy, is a total waste of time. Also largely a waste of time is overmarking work (please don't ever triple-mark[42]), therefore not giving it your full attention, and grading every piece of work[43]. Do you know what 95% of students do when you mark a piece of work and give it a letter or numbered grade? They read the grade, think, 'Oh good, I got a B', and close the book. What is much more beneficial, is going through a book, correcting key elements you are focusing on within that topic, be that

---

[41] Elliott, V., Randhawa, A., Ingram, J., Nelson-Addy, L., Griffin, C. and Baird, J.A. (2020). *Feedback: Practice Review*. London: Education Endowment Foundation.

[42] Dabell, J. (2018) *Educational Super-Fad: The Madness Of Triple Marking.* Available at: https://www.teachertoolkit.co.uk/2018/05/06/educational-fad-4/

[43] Elliot, V., Baird, J., Hopfenbeck, T., Ingram, J., Thompson, I., Usher, N., Zantout, M., Richardson, J., Coleman, R. (2016). *A Marked Improvement?* London: Education Endowment Foundation.

spelling, how to properly use a certain mathematical equation, or what the social and economic impacts of the American civil war were, and correcting those misunderstandings. If, through this process, you find that many of the students in a class have made the same mistake (*Abraham Lincoln: Vampire Hunter* may be good fun, but it should not be used as a trusted resource when it comes to studying the intricacies of the civil war), it is good practice to start the next lesson by revisiting these mistakes and correcting them as a class. This marking is then driving our future-teaching, we are actively addressing misconceptions, and we are ensuring our students are ready to move onto the next part of their learning. Delivering whole-class feedback, focused on something which most of the students in the room need extra work on, can also drastically cut down our marking time and save us from having to write the same thing in thirty workbooks. Once a misconception or mistake has become apparent, spend ten minutes at the start of the next lesson covering it again – rather than individually marking it in each book. It's important to do this as soon after the mistakes are made as possible, such as at the start of the very next lesson, as students are liable to forget something which took place weeks prior[44]. In this sense feedback must be both **meaningful**, and **timely**.

Should you be taking boxes of books home and marking every single night? The short answer is no. The UK government, and maybe more importantly, Ofsted, have no specific guidelines on the frequency, type or volume of book marking, and therefore there is no national expectation for

[44] Elliot, V., Baird, J., Hopfenbeck, T., Ingram, J., Thompson, I., Usher, N., Zantout, M., Richardson, J., Coleman, R. (2016). *A Marked Improvement?* London: Education Endowment Foundation.

you to have marked every piece of work in every book[45]. In fact, this would be a total waste of time, and I don't think it would be humanly possible to mark to this degree and have that marking be meaningful, or of any discernible quality. I advise marking less frequently, but to a higher quality. This will be somewhat driven by whole-school policy, but if you can mark each of your classes' work to a detailed degree, once a fortnight (maybe slightly more, maybe slightly less), while also engaging with those students in lessons and doing some live marking while teaching in smaller groups or one-to-one while working around your classrooms, I would argue you are delivering a good level of marked feedback. Much more so than someone who supposedly marks every day, by ticking, flicking, and stamping a grade or, even worse, a 'Well Done' stamp, at the bottom of each piece of work. Less frequent, **meaningful** marking is the way to go. And if you do find yourself marking and you look up and see its 6 o'clock at night, do yourself a favour and close those books. You can finish up tomorrow, the books will still be there.

Assessment

There are two types of assessment. Well, no. There are *lots* of types of assessments, but they tend to fall into two main categories: Formative Assessment and Summative Assessment.

---

[45] National Education Union. (2021) *Feedback and marking*. Available at: https://neu.org.uk/advice/feedback-and-marking

Formative Assessment, or 'Assessment for Learning', is on-going assessment you use with your students while they are being taught a topic[46] [47]. This can range from directed questioning, to homework, to quizzes, to even acting out a piece of learning, and these are often things we do naturally in our classrooms. It's how we tell, throughout the course of a lesson or topic, how well our students are understanding, learning, what's going well, and what we may need to spend extra time covering.

Summative Assessment is the process of evaluating the students' learning at the end of an agreed period, such as the end of a topic/term, and often takes the form of a more formal assessment, the dreaded *test*[48]. Summative Assessment usually gives us concrete data (more on that coming up) on how our students are performing.

Research tells us new teachers tend to have a preference for formative assessment over summative assessment[49], likely because it is more

---

[46] Coombs, A., DeLuca, C., LaPointe-McEwan, D. and Chalas, A. (2018) Changing approaches to classroom assessment: An empirical study across teacher career stages. *Teaching and Teacher Education*. 71 (1), p.134-144

[47] Gotwals, A. and Cisterna, D. (2022) Formative assessment practice progressions for teacher preparation: A framework and illustrative case. *Teaching and Teacher Education*. 110 (1), p.103-120

[48] Black, P. (2016) The role of assessment in pedagogy – And why validity matters. Ch.45, pp. 725–739 in D. Wyse, L. Hayward & J. Pandya (eds.) *The Sage Handbook of curriculum, pedagogy and assessment*. Sage: London

[49] Coombs, A., DeLuca, C., LaPointe-McEwan, D. and Chalas, A. (2018) Changing approaches to classroom assessment: An empirical study across teacher career stages. *Teaching and Teacher Education*. 71 (1), p.134-144

instantaneous and can be used, in real-time, to debunk misconceptions in the learning and correct common mistakes. There is an argument that summative assessment, which can take place weeks, if not months, after an initial piece of learning, does less to *teach* and correct these mistakes, focuses too heavily on students 'getting a grade', and can in some circumstances lead teachers to teach to pass an assessment as opposed to teaching towards holistic development[50]. But like it or not, both types of assessment are going to play a significant role in your teaching career. Should learning be centred around assessment, scoring students, and comparing them against each other? No. Is it? Often.

Exactly how assessment works in your school will depend on whole-school policy. Usually, formative assessment is down to you (and you may well be asked to evidence how/when you're doing it, so make sure you've worked some Challenge Grids into your lesson plans), and summative assessment is directed by the school, with set assessments which need to be taken by your students at set times. These set times often prelude a 'Data Deadline', a day when data collected all across the school must be submitted, analysed and jiggery-pokeried in time for upcoming reports.

If you are at a new or transitioning school, or one that may just not be particularly well organised when it comes to assessment, you may be in charge of putting together your own summative assessments. You should be directed on what your school wants, how often the students are to be assessed, and what they should be being assessed on, but usually these assessments will

[50] Koretz, D. (2017) *The Testing Charade: Pretending to Make Schools Better*. The University of Chicago Press: Chicago

follow a topic of work, and cover, with a range of different questioning styles, the content of the topic they have just completed. Older year groups may be expected to answer questions on topics they covered a longer time ago, or even on things you haven't covered with them, but which you would have expected them to have looked over in their own time. The thinking here being that a GCSE exam will cover topics they've studied for a 2-to-3-year-period, and that the retention and revision of knowledge is its own skill your students will have to practice.

I have mixed feelings about assessment, particularly summative, as do many teachers[51] [52]. It clearly has its place, our students do need to be prepared for GCSEs and A Levels, and any other exams they may sit. As well as assessing them on a particular topic's content, summative assessments give our students the experience of working under exam conditions, answering questions in a set timeframe, and experience in dealing with exam and revision pressures. In its simplest form, assessment, both formative and summative, tells us what our students know, what they don't yet know, and therefore can help us plan what needs covering going forwards[53]. However, do I want our students, young people with individual challenges, needs and, let's be honest, brilliances, to be put under frequent exam pressure? Do I want our schools to become 'exam factories', more concerned with results than the

---

[51] Christodoulou, D. (2017) *Making Good Progress? The Future of Assessment for Learning*. Oxford University Press: Oxford

[52] Kippers, W., Wolterinck, C., Schildkamp, K., Poortman, C., and Visscher, A. (2018) Teachers' views on the use of assessment for learning and data-based decision making in classroom practice. *Teaching and Teacher Education*. 75 (3), p.199-213

[53] Earle, S. (2021) Principles and purposes of assessment in the classroom. *Impact*. (12), p. 20–23

holistic development of their young people? No. This is perhaps controversial in the modern world, but I don't believe young people go to school to solely pass exams, and I'd strongly argue qualifications may not be the most important thing they gain from their time in education. Exams and qualifications are just one factor is the development and growth of young people. They have their place, but so does moral and social growth. So does the development of resilience and global citizenship. I believe it's important to teach a love of lifelong learning, rather than the knack of passing exams. Development **must** be holistic. Assessment is not inherently bad, certainly has its place within wider holistic development, and can be hugely beneficial when used correctly, but for this to happen it must be used purposefully and the results/feedback from these needs to be used productively to drive future learning[54]. Even if summative assessment is largely taken out of your hands at your school, and driven by wider whole-school policies, I implore you to ensure you're using the assessments as productively as you can, and that their results are used to guide your future teaching and your students' future learning, rather than to tell a student, 'You've got a B'.

As with everything in schools, it's about balance. A lot of that balance, especially with summative assessment, is likely to be taken out of your hands and driven by school policy, but even when this is the case, you will have *some* say on how proactively you use the results and data. As for formative assessment, you will need to factor this into your lessons regularly and be mindful and attentive of what you learn from it to drive your future planning

---

[54] Koretz, D. (2017) *The Testing Charade: Pretending to Make Schools Better.* The University of Chicago Press: Chicago

to make sure there are no (or at least *fewer*) gaps in what your students are taking away from your lessons. Try to make this formative assessment fun (as fun as a maths quiz can be), with points and rewards, working it into your lessons in a low-key, relaxed, way. This is one way to ensure we're still getting the data we require to drive our future teaching, but where it doesn't feel like our students are continuously being *tested*.

The next question: What happens with the results of all this assessment?

Data

Collecting data, data deadlines, evidencing learning, Target Grades (TAGs), Working At Grades (WAGs), and spreadsheets; these are the bugbears of many a teacher. Most teachers get into the professional with a certain level of idealism, we want to spark and inspire young minds. We want to holistically build up the next generation, not just academically, but socially, emotionally, and morally. And, in truth, many of us didn't want to end up office-drones, filling up spreadsheets with numbers. Guess what? Your assessments lead to data, and that data needs processing. Stap yourself in for what I call: 'The least fun part of teaching'.

I'm going on a slight tangent here. *Do* some teachers go into the profession loving data? Many larger schools will have multiple Deputy or Assistant Heads, and often one of these will take charge of 'data'. They usually no longer teach, instead spending their days receiving and calculating student data, spat out of some end-of-topic assessments, working out students' current working grades, and making predictions of where they are going to be by the end of year 11 or year 13. They have an office job. And I'm *very* sceptical of these people. Always have been. I don't believe many teachers get into this career-path with an end goal of wanting an office role. I dare say, if you *did* want an office 'data' job, many young graduates can find one early-on in their careers with a higher starting salary than that of a teacher, and without the hassle of going through teacher training, ECT years, and the day-to-day challenges teaching throws at us. Maybe it's these challenges that wore them down? Maybe they wake up one day (it's normally a man or woman in their 50s) and think, 'Teaching's a young man's/woman's game. But it's all I've known. How can I get a nice, quiet, corner office? Ah – I can oversee... data!'. Maybe I'm wrong (it wouldn't be the first time), but it's always made me wonder.

Pondering aside, your summative assessments will need to be marked, this will lead to data, and this data, in turn, needs to be processed (*'needs to be'* being a debatable term – is it clear yet that I'm not *massively* keen on an overuse of assessment and data collection?) and turned into some variety of target grade. Different schools have different lingo, you may be aware of TAGs, WAGs, or something else entirely, but it normally boils down to the same thing – a grade you believe a student is working at currently, and a grade a student is expected to achieve by the end of their course, be that GCSE or A Level, or something else. These grades are often put into reports and sent home to parents/carers at set times throughout the year.

Each school will have their own methods of collecting and processing data. I've uploaded results onto programs such as Doddle, SIMs, Solar, Evidence for Learning and good old Microsoft Excel, and probably a few others I've forgotten about. Each system will run slightly differently, but largely has the same purpose- to record assessment data, and sometimes convert that data into those elusive grades. Sometimes that's done manually. Which program you use, and how often you collect data, will depend on your school, but one thing I've found across many different schools is that the data deadline is a **big deal**. The name here again may differ, Data Points, Data Drops, Transfer Deadline Day, but that deadline for when your data must be uploaded is normally a hard deadline. With that in mind, make sure your students have sat their assessments with time to spare before the data deadline so that you've got time to mark and collect the results. That way, you can upload your data in advance of any deadline, and save yourself added hassle (which is something we're all trying to avoid in schools).

Parents' Evening

Parents' evening…Duh…Duh…Duhhh (the ominous sound of crashing thunder and lightning). Periodically, usually twice or three times a year, you will come face to face with the parents and carers of your students, and be expected to discuss their progress, behaviour, and how they're generally getting on. You will also be expected to answer questions on their work, next steps and expectations, and anything else particularly quizzical parents can think to ask. With parents sat across a table from you, there is nowhere to run and little opportunity to check an answer with a mentor or colleague, so make sure you're going in prepared (however, if you really don't know an answer, a reasonable parent *should* be happy for you to say you need to double-check, and get back to them with a phone-call or email the next day). For many a new teacher, parents' evenings can be a scary prospect, but we're going to go over why they're really an opportunity for you to make integral links between your students' school and home lives, and why you should go into them with nothing to fear!

When going into a parents' evening, remember one thing: we all (should) want the same outcome. Parents and teachers should be working together to ensure the young person involved is getting the best opportunities, and developing towards their potential. Nervous early career teachers sometimes look at parents' evenings as if they're a battle, parents vs me, a hellfire of questions will rain, 'Why isn't my child predicted the highest grades?', 'What grades will my child achieve, *exactly*?', 'Where will my child be in five years from now?', 'Why aren't you doing more to ensure my child becomes a judge/ Prime Minister/ an astronaut?'. I'm striving to be as truthful as possible in this guide, and yes, you may face some tricky questions from parents. **But this is not the norm**. 99% of parents are supportive, want the best for their children, and are appreciative of all the work you put in for them. Remember this fact when going into your parents' evenings. The one or two who may give you a hard time? The ones that expect their children to be performing academically above and beyond what you think is reasonably expectable, or the ones who want you to effectively be a one-to-one tutor and ensure their darling makes it into Oxbridge? Be truthful, be up-front, and have your data and workbooks with you, so that you can confidently evidence where their child is currently working at. And, if all else fails, be courteous, polite (even when they're pushing you to your limits), and explain you will need to check their query with your Head of Department, or similar, and get back to them with an email or phone-call the next day.

So, how do parents' evenings work? Guidance should be provided by your school, but normally there will be a set evening, and each student attending should book a timeslot with you in advance. If your school is not arranging this booking system, I **highly advise** putting one in place yourself. Especially if you work in a larger school and are planning on seeing many different students. It's important you know which student is seeing you when. Remember, you'll strive to ensure you don't have a forgotten middle section of students in your classroom, but you may still have the names of three-hundred-odd students floating around in your head, and the name of that one Year 8 boy who you teach for one hour a week, and who barely makes a peep, might just escape you at the precise moment he's sat opposite you with his mum and dad. However, if you know he's booked a 5:45 pm slot with you, you can check your own corresponding list, and see *exactly* who's meant to be sat across from you at quarter to six. Even better, because you were pre-empting his arrival, you've already put his books out and you've opened his data up on your laptop. You're ready to go! This doesn't *always* work. Sometimes students and parents will turn up when it isn't their timeslot. Other teachers have overrun, or underrun, or someone else hasn't turned up and they've noticed you're free- but it's still a helpful tool, and may just get you out of the sticky situation of asking, 'And you are, again?'

Once you've put together your booking list, and you know who is attending parents' evening, prepare everything you may need to discuss and evidence your students' work. Have students' workbooks ready, and make sure your marking is up to date (at the very least, make sure the last few pieces of work are marked and ready for you to show and discuss).

Have the student data open and ready-to-go on your computer, or print out copies of progress reports and assessment results ready for reference (see, that data does have some benefit after all!). Make sure any target or predicted grades you've assigned to a student correlate with the assessment results and bookwork you've got to show. Be able to confidently say, 'They're working towards a high grade because...' or, 'The reason this grade isn't as high as we'd like is because...'. When it comes to those students who aren't achieving grades as high as they are expected to, it may be a good idea to pre-empt the parents with a phone call prior to the meeting. This can limit any awkward conversations/questions on the night, gives the parents extra time to process any feelings about the news, and can even give you a better idea of what to expect when you meet. Are they supportive of both their child, the work you are doing, and are they willing to work with you to help support their child to raise their output? Or are they devastated by the news, assured the school and teaching staff are failing their child, and ready to make their feelings heard? (again, unlikely, and the *vast* minority – but it does happen and it can only be beneficial to be forewarned!).

Have a timer with you. This doesn't necessarily need to be a phone alarm set to go off every ten minutes, but do keep an eye on the clock, and when time is up, very politely say, 'I need to see the next parent now, have you got any last questions?', and, 'please feel free to email or call me at any time if you'd like to discuss your child further'. Some parents will happily drag on for an hour. If you're seeing lots of students in an evening, this will (clearly) become unmanageable very quickly. On that note, parents' evenings are often long events, even if all parents stick to their ten-minute slot, arrive on time, and don't ask any difficult questions (the trifactor, if only all parent's evenings went like this). Bring snacks and a flask of tea (or alternative) with you. The last thing you want is a dry mouth and a rumbling stomach, and trust me, you will be talking *a lot* during parents' evenings. Keep those energy levels up!

Lastly, remember why we do parents' evenings. In providing the best support for our young people, it is vital we build strong links between home and school. I don't have any data to back this up, call it more of a gut-feeling, but home/school links seemed to have worsened in the last decade or so. Class sizes **are** growing[55], and with the increasing pressures on teachers and their growing workloads, time is literally running out to make frequent meaningful contact with our students' parents and carers. But it's so important we don't allow these links to shrivel up and die. For our students to have the best chances of success, whatever form that may take, support needs to be provided from all angles, both at home and in school, and preferably we'd all be singing from the same hymn sheet. Use parents' evenings as an opportunity to familiarise yourself with your students' parents and carers. Show them all

---

[55] HM Government. (2022) *Schools, pupils and their characteristics*. Available at: https://explore-education-statistics.service.gov.uk/find-statistics/school-pupils-and-their-characteristics

the things their children are achieving, and make them aware of any areas where they require more support. Get the parents onside, and you will have a powerful tool going forward to support the future teaching of your students.

Phone Calls Home

Parent's evenings can be fantastic (they can also be a little scary at first, and that's fine!), but the reality is that you may only see a student's parents once per year, and even at schools with fewer students or a higher drive for teacher/parent relationships, you will probably only see parents in an official capacity three times a year at most (not including times such as pick-ups and drop-offs, which can be great opportunities to exchange quick information and continue to build those school to home relationships).

The relationships between school and home are hugely important. A student's development must be holistic, and for the best outcomes, support needs to be coordinated and available from all areas of a young person's life. You can't control the support your students receive from home, and you may very well come across times when you find it isn't readily available (which makes what we do even more essential), but you **can** control your input in building links between school and home, and offer support, advice, and intervention such as home-learning (worksheets, booklets, access to websites), to further support a young person.

This is where phone calls home come into play. There are, rightly or wrongly, hundreds if not thousands of parents up and down the country who assume a phone call from their child's school will always be a negative experience. They dread the thought of seeing the school's number flash up on their phone, they wonder, 'What has happened now?', and may go as far as avoiding the call. This can quickly start a negative cycle of parents then having a negative perception of the school and education itself (possibly entwined with feelings from their own time in education), which can lead to a negative home/school relationship developing, and parents even going as far as to become less willing to support their child's education as a result. This may sound extreme, but I can promise you this happens more regularly than you'd care to think. Thankfully, there is an alternative to this scenario: **The Positive Phone Call Home**.

Break any developing cycles of negativity, and support positive links between the school and the home, by regularly ringing parents when their child has done something fantastic in your classroom. By doing so you will also solidify and strengthen those relationships with parents which you've begun developing during Parents' Evenings. Research from Harvard

University has shown that positive communication between teachers and parents/carers can increase rates of students completing their homework by 40% and students' in-class participation by 15%[56]. Parents genuinely love to hear how well their children are doing, our students crave the positive attention, and we all give more and work harder when we feel appreciated and valued[57]. These phone calls will also reflect positively on you and the school. We're busy, and many teachers may not take the time to make these positive calls, but when you do it shows how attentive, caring, and invested, you are as a practitioner. Parents will remember these calls, and they will be grateful to you for making them.

What do we do if we need to relay some less positive news to a student's home? What if behaviours in lessons are directly impacting the learning of other students and we need support from parents in managing this? First off, there is no shame and no problem with going to parents with behaviour issues, as with positive support, behaviour management is at its most successful when it is holistic and coming from all angles. However, before ringing home with bad news, I would always advise considering the following:

- **What Potential Solutions Could You Put In Place?** Parents, by and large, will be less receptive to reports of their child misbehaving when

---

[56] Kraft, M., and Dougherty, S., M. (2013) The effect of teacher-family communication on student engagement: Evidence from a randomized field experiment. *Journal of Research on Educational Effectiveness*. 6 (3), p. 199 - 222

[57] Gregory, K. (2011) The importance of employee satisfaction. *The Journal of the Division of Business & Information Management*. 5 (1), p. 29-37

no next steps are suggested. It's perfectly acceptable to ring home for advice, but try to have a suggestion of, 'We could try an end-of-week reward for positive behaviour', or, 'The school policy is to sanction the behaviour by taking away breaktimes'. Take onboard their feedback on these ideas and work with them to find potentially successful solutions.

- **Focus On The Positives As Well As The Negatives:** Sometimes it may feel like hard work, but if we look hard enough, we **will** find positives alongside the negatives in each of our students (and in most the positives will far outweigh the negatives). Show a parent that you're looking at the whole picture, and not focused solely on the negatives, by starting a conversation praising something constructive a student has achieved. This could be a piece of work, an example of good manners, or even just a breaktime or lesson where nothing went particularly wrong. Explain that, with support and by making the right choices, the student can have a much more positive time at school than they may currently be having.

- **Be Clear On What You Want To Say:** I've spoken about how teaching can be a challenging profession at times, and it can also be an emotional one. We put a lot into our jobs, and rightly or wrongly, we sometimes feel behaviours and outcomes are personal, based on how much we've poured in. We're human, and these feelings, from time-to-time, are fine to have (although please try not to take behaviours personally, and make sure to talk to a mentor or colleague if you are finding it tough). But, and I strongly recommend this, do not make a phone call home when you're feeling emotional and overly invested. Even if the call needs to wait till the next day, after the initial behaviours, ring with a calm head and be clear and concise on what the issues were, what solutions you've considered, and how the parents can potentially support you and the student. Parents will **not** appreciate a moan, they will be much more responsive to clear, concise, feedback, and an opportunity to brainstorm and reach solutions together which benefit the young person involved.

The Rest

A teacher's mind is a little bit like a juggler, trying to keep many different balls in the air. Your main concerns, your biggest balls (stop giggling at the back of the room!), should be your students and your lessons. You'll have balls flying around your head with thoughts about starters, main tasks, and plenaries, you'll have ideas about building positive relationships and setting classroom standards. You'll then have balls focused on working within the parameters of your school, and any whole-school approaches and policies you need to abide by. But as teachers, we aren't juggling just three or four balls. We're experienced, world-class, jugglers, and we're often juggling twenty, thirty, if not more, balls in our minds. Many of these balls are what I call 'The Rest'. Often times these are things we don't need to actively use on an everyday basis, and sometimes they are, but either way, they are still important aspects of the holistic world of teaching which we need to be prepared and ready for. Here lies, The Rest.

The Teacher Standards

The Teacher Standards. What are they? What do they mean? And, most importantly, do they matter?

The New Teacher's Survival Guide

According to our government, the Teacher Standards are the **minimum** requirements for a teacher's practice and conduct[58]. Think of them a little like the standards you set in your own classroom for yourself and your students. These are the standards the government sets for you, and it is expected that you meet them at all times.

Sounds serious right? Well, they are. And to answer my earlier question: Do they matter? They do. But let me pose another question: If you were to select a teacher at random right now from your school, and asked them to recite the Teacher Standards by heart, would they be able to do it? Probably not.

These standards are both important, and something very few teachers actively think about on a day-to-day basis. Ultimately, you will meet these standards without thinking too deeply about them, because they are the basic pillars of teaching, and you will be a high-quality educator. However, if you're new to the profession, it's a good idea to read up and get your head around them, and if you're *very* new, and still at the stage of considering teaching as a career path, they're a good indicator as to what is expected in teaching.

With no further ado, allow me to introduce the Teacher Standards[59]:

[58] HM Government. (2021) *Teachers' Standards*. Available at:
https://www.gov.uk/government/publications/teachers-standards
[59] Department for Education. (2011) *Teachers' Standards: Overview*. Available at:
https://assets.publishing.service.gov.uk/government/uploads/system/uploads/attachment_data/file/665522/Teachers_standard_information.pdf

Part One: Teaching.

A teacher must,

    1. 'Set high expectations which inspire, motivate and challenge pupils.'

Both with your classroom expectations and with your high-quality lesson planning, you will push your students to be the best they can be and to achieve the highest potentials you can reasonably expect from them. What students can achieve in your room will vary wildly, for some this may mean high grades in all of their GCSEs, for others it may be that you inspire them to grow into mature, thoughtful, well-rounded, citizens. For many, it will be both these things. It's about challenging your students to an appropriate level and making sure they meet their own potentials. This comes from your planning, the differentiation you set within your lessons, and your ability to inspire and motivate by setting good examples.

    2. 'Promote good progress and outcomes by pupils.'

You will get to know your students, you will refuse to have a forgotten middle section in your classroom, and by knowing your students you will be confident in their attainment levels, how they are progressing in your classroom, and how you can best guide them to their highest potential outcomes. A lot of this will be academic, and you will assess and keep appropriate data to show how your students are progressing, but many of these outcomes may not be academic. Helping a young person develop into a polite and attentive individual is an incredibly positive outcome. It's all about guiding your students to be the best they can be.

3.   'Demonstrate good subject and curriculum knowledge.'

If you're teaching biology, you need a strong subject knowledge of biology. You *probably* have a biology degree, so that's a good start! However, you will also need to know what's on the biology curriculum, and be confident that you can convey your higher-level understanding of your topic to much younger students in a way they can fully access and engage with. It's amazing, even when we become specialists in our areas of expertise, how much of the basics we learnt in school ourselves can be forgotten. If you're starting a new school in September, take a little time in the summer to brush up on your subject knowledge.

As well as your area of expertise, you will also need to be confident in your basic maths and English (lucky you, maths and English teachers, two birds with one stone). It's all our jobs to make sure our students are proficient in their basic literacy and arithmetic, and as I mentioned in 'The Starter', it's a good idea to make sure we're working cross-curricular elements into all of our lessons.

4.   'Plan and teach well-structured lessons.'

All the subject knowledge in the world is no good if you can't find an effective way of imparting it to your students. There are many different ways of teaching, and you will need to use many different methods throughout your career, so go back over 'Lesson Planning', try out a few different approaches, and make sure you consistently work starters, main tasks and plenaries into your lessons. As you get to know your students, you will find out how they best learn, and you can plan and differentiate to their strengths. Also, and sometimes we need reminding of this, your teaching will continuously improve with practice. I'm a much better teacher now than I was when I started, and I like to think in some small way I'm a better teacher now than I was even last week. Keep planning, keep teaching, and keep improving.

5.   'Adapt teaching to respond to the strengths and needs of all pupils.'

At the risk of repeating myself, get to know your students and teach to their specific needs and strengths. Be confident of any SENDs in your classroom, any EAL, or PP – and adjust your teaching, seating plans, and activities accordingly for these students. Make concreate adjustments within your lesson planning and in your seating plans (students with SEND or additional learning needs at the front, for example), so that you can evidence you're doing all you can to improve **every** student's learning (we don't do these things to evidence, we do them because we're high-quality teachers and it's the right thing to do. But, y'know, teaching in the real world requires a certain amount of, 'Look here, it's written down!'). At the same time, push your higher attainers on with extension tasks and higher thinking scenarios. Again, it's about all of your students meeting whatever their potential may be.

6. 'Make accurate and productive use of assessment.'

Include formative assessment opportunities in all your lessons, and have your students undertake summative assessments at the appropriate times. I've spoken in 'Assessment' about my preferences when it comes to assessing our young people, and you will need to make a decision on how/when you choose to assess your students, but it is important that they have regular opportunities to display their learning, and that you are aware of what has actually been *learnt* in your classroom, so that you can plan and teach accordingly. When you do assess, log and submit your data on time, and most importantly, provide feedback to your students on any assessment they've taken. This may be in the form of larger written feedback for tests and assignments, but it may also be a short verbal response to a student's answer in class. Praise them when they get an answer correct, and inform them on how to improve if they've made a mistake. That's how we learn for next time.

7. 'Manage behaviour effectively to ensure a good and safe learning environment.'

Set your classroom expectations, develop your relationships, build a reputation, have both praises and consequences in place, and most importantly, be fair and consistent while doing all these things. Go into that classroom knowing exactly what the school's behaviour policy is, and what you should do if behaviours in your room are leading to an environment that may not be entirely safe or adequate for learning.

8. 'Fulfil wider professional responsibilities.'

This one's a bit of a cop-out which effectively means, 'and do everything else you may be asked to do within a school.' Complete rudimentary admin, keep parents in the loop through regular contact on-top of set parent's evenings, be proactive in undertaking CPD (Continuing Professional Development) to develop your teaching ability. It's not *all* nonsense, *some* of that admin has a wider purpose and feeds into student progress data, we know parents need to be informed of their child's development, and you *should* always be looking to develop your teaching practice – but a lot of 'wider responsibilities' will end up being admin, evidencing, and attending meetings which *really* could have just been emails, and that is, unfortunately, another truth of teaching.

Part Two: Personal and Professional Conduct.

This part is interesting. As teachers, we are expected to, 'uphold public trust in the profession and maintain high standards of ethics and behaviour, [both] within and **outside** school'[60]. There is a grey area on what schools can and cannot enforce on your life outside of the classroom, but this is something we shall try to unpick.

---

[60] Department for Education. (2011) *Teachers' Standards: Overview.* Available at: https://assets.publishing.service.gov.uk/government/uploads/system/uploads/attachment_data/file/665522/Teachers_standard_information.pdf

---

PART TWO: PERSONAL AND PROFESSIONAL CONDUCT

A teacher is expected to demonstrate consistently high standards of personal and professional conduct. The following statements define the behaviour and attitudes which set the required standard for conduct throughout a teacher's career.

- Teachers uphold public trust in the profession and maintain high standards of ethics and behaviour, within and outside school, by:
  - treating pupils with dignity, building relationships rooted in mutual respect, and at all times observing proper boundaries appropriate to a teacher's professional position
  - having regard for the need to safeguard pupils' well-being, in accordance with statutory provisions
  - showing tolerance of and respect for the rights of others
  - not undermining fundamental British values, including democracy, the rule of law, individual liberty and mutual respect, and tolerance of those with different faiths and beliefs
  - ensuring that personal beliefs are not expressed in ways which exploit pupils' vulnerability or might lead them to break the law.

- Teachers must have proper and professional regard for the ethos, policies and practices of the school in which they teach, and maintain high standards in their own attendance and punctuality.

- Teachers must have an understanding of, and always act within, the statutory frameworks which set out their professional duties and responsibilities.

Figure 11- Teacher Standards, Part Two: Personal And Professional Conduct (Department for Education, 2011)

Figure 11 details The DoE's (Department for Education) (2011) key points for maintaining public trust and high standards within the profession. These points, in my opinion, are perfectly reasonable, and important, qualities we would expect to see in good teachers. We want to see mutual respect in our classrooms, we **must** safeguard our student's wellbeing (see: **Safeguarding**), we need to all show tolerance and promote British values in our schools, and (hopefully this goes without saying) we should never express views in our classrooms with may exploit students' vulnerabilities or lead them to break the law.

The DoE go on to state that we as teachers should have proper and professional regard for the ethos, policies, and practises of our schools, that we should maintain good attendance and punctuality, and that we should understand and act within the frameworks of our professional duties and responsibilities (the Teacher Standards we have been going over).

Be on time, be respectful (rules we would surely expect to see in any workplace), and remember that we are working with young minds and that we must make sure we are being appropriate and feeding their moral and social growth as well as their academic. This last one may lead to some differences from other workplaces. Certain jokes or language that you have made and used while working with adults may not be appropriate and welcome within a school. This again seems fair enough to me, it is the job, and you will need to exercise your common sense and teacher judgment when deciding what is and isn't appropriate (but as a rule, stay away from anything with the potential to be *risqué*; that's sex, drugs, drinking, anything illegal, or anything downright stupid. But, just to confuse the matter, this may not apply in an appropriate PSHE lesson, such as one on the dangers and laws around drug use, and that's where common sense comes into play).

This all seems simple enough on paper, but as is often the case, it is the interpretation of the rules which can confuse matters. Here's an example for you, and a question I have been posed in a teacher meeting: 'As teachers, can we be seen to be drunk and disorderly out in public, outside of school hours?'

Let's be a little more specific: You're out drinking with friends in the town in which you also happen to teach. You're doing nothing illegal, but you've had one too many, and now you and your friends are posing for photographs outside of the local kebab shop, wearing traffic cones as hats. It's outside school hours, and it's the weekend, so any potential hangover wouldn't impact your next day's teaching, and you even intend to put the cones right back where you found them after the photo-op. However, some of your students, *and their parents*, live locally and would recognise you behaving in this way. Are you currently upholding public trust in the profession, which we know has to be maintained both inside and outside of school?

There is no definitive answer for this scenario in the Teacher Standards. I have come across teachers who have said that they believe it is inappropriate to be seen out drunk, at any time, while holding the position of a classroom teacher. I know plenty of *other* teachers who like to get sloshed most weekends. I can only give my honest opinion here, but I would argue strongly that you are allowed to go out and enjoy your free time away from school in any manner you see fit (within the confines of the law). I myself am not against a few Indian Pale Ales down my local, and I wouldn't be part of any profession which took this simple pleasure away from me. Where I choose to draw the line, and this isn't in the Teacher Standards *per se*, it comes down to my own professional judgment, is that I wouldn't come to school with a hangover (just *imagine* dealing with a particularly loud, screechy, group), and I wouldn't recommend putting any inappropriate images (drunk, bikinis, anything potentially dangerous/ridiculous) on social media. If you are on social media, I'd strongly recommend having your privacy settings turned up to the max ('Turn it up to 11' – Spinal Tap anyone?), and that you use an alternative name for your online profile. Kids **will** try and Google you, and you don't want to be easy to find. Going back to my hypothetical scenario with the traffic cone on your head: You are still allowed to go out and have a laugh with your friends (as much as many of our students could never imagine such a thing), but you really wouldn't want the photographic evidence to be seen by your students. Do go out, do enjoy yourself, perhaps **don't** allow a picture of yourself with a traffic cone on your head to do the rounds. Remember that *reputation* you're building around your school? A drunken photo on social media is a quick way to kiss goodbye to that.

Safeguarding

What is safeguarding?

According to the Department of Education (2022) safeguarding and the promotion of our young people's welfare consists of[61]:

- Protecting children from maltreatment.
- Preventing the impairment of children's mental and physical health or development.
- Ensuring that children grow up in circumstances consistent with the provision of safe and effective care.

---

[61] Department of Education (2022) *Keeping children safe in education 2022.* Department of Education: London

- Taking action to enable all children to have the best outcomes.

Part 2 of the Teacher Standards makes specific reference to safeguarding our students' wellbeing[62]. Furthermore, government stature says that **everyone** working in schools must understand their safeguarding responsibilities, and **everyone**, from teachers to dinner supervisors, and all in between, has a responsibility in safeguarding and promoting positive wellbeing for the young people we work with[63]. Safeguarding might be the most important thing we do, above even providing a high standard of education. If our students aren't safe, how can they be in the correct mindset to learn? I *could* then, have opened this book with a chapter on safeguarding. It could be *strongly* argued that the safety and wellbeing of our students are our main priority, above all else. But I've chosen not to, and my reasoning for this is as follows: During your trainee and ECT years 90% of your time and effort will be focused on planning and delivering high-quality lessons. That's the reason you've become a teacher (probably), and you're still learning your trade. 10% of your time and effort will cover everything else, including safeguarding. I say this not to belittle safeguarding, which is incredibly important, but to be truthful and give you an honest reflection of an early teaching career. With this in mind, when it comes to safeguarding in your early career, you must be vigilant, but you must also know (100% without doubt) who to approach and who can support you if you have a safeguarding concern. Safeguarding is a

---

[62] Department for Education. (2011) *Teachers' Standards: Overview.* Available at: https://assets.publishing.service.gov.uk/government/uploads/system/uploads/attachment_data/file/665522/Teachers_standard_information.pdf
[63] Department of Education (2022) *Keeping children safe in education 2022.* Department of Education: London

whole-school responsibility, and there **will** be someone in your school whose job it is to support you if you have a safeguarding concern and aren't sure how to proceed with it.

In your early years that will be the most important thing you need to know regarding safeguarding: **who you should approach and tell if you have a safeguarding concern**. I cannot stress enough, the worst possible thing you can do if you have a concern is to keep that information to yourself. Hopefully, your school has made it clear to you who your DSLs (Designated Safeguarding Leads) are, the specific staff members who should be informed of, and help deal with, safeguarding concerns, and you should also have a mentor or Head of Department in place who can help/direct you if you are ever unsure. It's entirely acceptable, and I think healthy, for you to be largely focused on your teaching early on. Even as more experienced teachers, we can't have the wellbeing of every student weighing down on our shoulders, all of the time, it would quickly become unmanageable and, frankly, overbearing – and this is something the Department of Education advises us on. Building a picture of any safeguarding concerns is everyone's responsibility, and no single staff member can be fully aware of, and deal with, a student's entire needs and circumstances[64] (physically, you cannot monitor that student 24 hours a day). It is a group effort. But as it is everyone's responsibility, we must all be vigilant. Don't ever feel you're alone if you do become aware of an issue or disclosure, seek out the proper support, and communicate with colleagues to build a better picture of any issues a student

---

[64] Department of Education (2022) *Keeping children safe in education 2022*. Department of Education: London

may be having. You may have noticed a small thing, a bruise on the arm for example, and it might be nothing, it might be a sports injury. But if a colleague has seen another bruise, or a change in behaviour, or even had a disclosure from that young person, then your small observation could go a long way to building a much better picture and getting that student the support they need. It isn't about solving the world's problems single-handedly, but it is about being aware, getting to know the students in your classes, and noticing any changes which could be cause for concern. I'll repeat myself at the risk of boring you, there are many things to know regarding safeguarding, but most importantly, if you have a concern: **tell someone**. Preferably you'd go straight to a DSL, but if ever unsure, just go to a senior member of staff and tell them. It's a team effort!

So, what sort of things do you need to be looking out for? It's an extensive list, including but not limited to[65]:

- **Physical Abuse** – any physical violence or undue force which has been used on a young person. Signs of physical abuse and assault may include new or unusual marks, bruises, burns, or broken bones. Another sign may be a young person trying to cover up these results of physical abuse with heavily applied make-up or clothing e.g. refusing to take off a long-sleeved jacket in warmer weather or get changed for a PE lesson.

---

[65] Department of Education (2022) *Keeping children safe in education 2022.* Department of Education: London

- **Emotional Abuse** – emotional abuse may include, amongst other things, undue and consistent criticism, belittling, gaslighting (manipulating or causing a young person to question their own sanity through the use of consistent abuse and undermining), or isolating of a young person, such as keeping them away from their friends or other family members. Signs of a young person experiencing emotional abuse may include depression, feelings of worthlessness, or withdrawal from social situations.

- **Sexual Abuse and Child Sexual Exploitation (CSE)** – the act of forcing or manipulating a minor into sexual activities. Sexual abuse and CSE includes both penetrative intercourse and non-penetrative sexual behaviour such as masturbation or kissing, or the sharing of sexualised images/videos. Signs of sexual abuse may include a young person having an unexplained knowledge of sexualised language or ideas, or having new unaccounted-for possessions or money which may be the result of 'gifts' from grooming.

- **Neglect** – a failure to meet a young person's basic needs, malnutrition, uncleanliness, and/or emotional needs not being met. A young person could potentially be at risk of malnutrition if they have lost a considerable amount of weight in a short period of time, and/or have much less body mass than their peers.

- **Child Criminal Exploitation (CCE)** – CCE involves young people being forced or manipulated into transporting drugs or money, theft, or committing violent acts. Part of this may include 'County Lines', the process of manipulating or forcing a young person to sell drugs or commit other illegal acts in other parts of the UK. Young people involved in this process may unexpectedly have more money/possessions themselves, or show signs associated with emotional abuse.

- **Female Genital Mutilation (FGM)** – the act of mutilating female genitalia, such as cutting or injuring the genitalia, for no medical purpose. This act is often performed as part of misguided cultural or religious practices, and can take place outside of the UK. Signs of a young person who has suffered from FGM may include the young person being in constant pain, bleeding, suffering from incontinence or asking to use the toilet more frequently, and associated mental health impacts such as depression. These ailments may follow an unexplained absence from school, when the young person may have been taken out of the country.

- **Mental Health Abuse** – any form of abuse may lead to a young person experiencing mental health issues, such as depression or post-traumatic stress disorder. This can lead to a young person acting out of character, erratically, or being withdrawn and/or seeming hopeless.

- **Peer on peer Abuse** – bullying and abuse between two or more young people. This may be physical, verbal or emotional, and may take place in or outside of school, or online. Often with bullying, these behaviours continue for extended periods of time and may be the result of a group of multiple young people becoming fixated on a smaller group of, or just one, other(s).

Every member of staff in a school needs to have read The Department of Education's (2022) '*Keeping Children Safe in Education*' document (or latest equivalent), which will give further detail on what specifically to look out for in a safeguarding concern[66]. A lot of the clues though, come down to changes in a young person, such as looking or behaving differently than usual. It may be that they've become withdrawn, or that they're wearing enough make-up that it could be hiding marks or bruises. This isn't always the case, and sometimes our young people will make changes to their personalities or appearances solely because they're growing up and discovering who they might want to be in their teenage and adult lives – but if you notice any stark changes, especially one that gives you a gut-feeling of concern, let a DSL know straight away.

Disclosures

Sometimes we may spot signs of potential abuse and report these to our DSLs, but other times a student may come directly to us and make a disclosure. What do we do if a student comes to us at the end of a day and tells us of something potentially shocking and horrible which is taking place in their lives?

- **Listen** – allow the student to tell you their concern. At this point, try not to ask questions and don't put any words in their mouth. It's vital

---

[66] Department of Education (2022) *Keeping children safe in education 2022.* Department of Education: London

the school knows what the student is saying took place, from their point of view.

- **Reassure** – make sure the student knows they are in a safe environment and that they are doing the right thing by sharing any fears or concerns with you. Reassure them it's our job to help them, not just academically, but also in matters concerning their wellbeing.

- **Be Honest** – let the student know you want to hear them, and that it's important they talk to you if they have an issue. But, you must be honest and tell them you **cannot** keep secrets. If they disclose a safeguarding concern to you, you will need to pass this on. Let the student know this and assure them this is an important step to getting the correct support for them.

- **Keep a Record** – You may choose to make a short-hand record of the conversation while it's taking place, or to focus on listening and then write up the conversation afterwards, but you must make a record of what's been said. Write down exactly what's been said to you, not your interpretation or feelings on the matter. Most schools now will have an online platform or program where safeguarding concerns can be securely written up.

- **Tell a Designated Safeguarding Lead** – Even if you've already written up and uploaded the concern onto an online safeguarding platform, go and directly tell a DSL if you've received a disclosure of a safeguarding concern. Make sure they are aware. They may also advise you on any next steps you will need to take.

O, We're Going To Ibiza! (Holidays)

Right back at the start of this guide, I asked you to write down the reason you wanted to become a teacher. Hopefully, part of your reasoning was about wanting to work with, inspire, and teach young people, but I wouldn't begrudge anyone who'd also mentioned the holidays. For me, as a geography teacher by trade, seeing other parts of the world is a hugely important aspect of my life, and the summer holiday offers me the time and opportunity to do that in a way most other jobs couldn't. Teachers, on average, work 195 days per year, compared to 227 for the average office worker in this country[67]. That equates to 170 days off (including weekends) per year. Or does it? Well, that entirely depends on your definition of a 'day off'. You will, on average, not be in school for 170 days a year – but I can guarantee you will be working some, if not, *quite a lot*, of those.

Exactly how much you work in your time outside of school is up to you, and the pressures of your school. There is no getting around some of it; all of our planning, marking, making of resources, and everything else, cannot be squeezed into the working day, where mostly our time is taken up by actually teaching (who'd have thought it?). But you *will* have some control over how much time you choose to put in after hours and on days off, and I recommend having a serious think early on about how many hours you're willing to put into the job. I don't know if the average teacher works more hours than the average office worker. We certainly get more days off on

---

[67] Department of Education. (2022) *Get into teaching: salaries and benefits.* Available at: https://getintoteaching.education.gov.uk/salaries-and-benefits

paper, but then if you're working more than eight hours a day (sometimes a few more), and half a day Saturday (a very real possibility), plus half of all your 'holiday time' e.g. one week of the two week Christmas break, then it may very well equate to more time overall. The time you spend working outside of the classroom will also change throughout your teaching career, with, as mentioned previously, more hours usually being put in at the start, as you create lessons and resources which won't need making from scratch again the second time around (this is, of course, until you climb the ladder to Head of Year or Head of Department, and find your responsibilities and workload suddenly multiplying again). Ultimately, we shouldn't go into the job worrying whether we're working more or less than our friends in other career paths (if you're in teaching for the money or *just* the holidays, you might end up a little disappointed), but at the same time you don't want to be working the equivalent of two full-time jobs, because you will just end up burning out and will probably leave the profession (remember that drop-out rate?).

I love teaching, I hope I've made that clear throughout this guide, but I am also a realist. I attended a training session early on in my teacher training where a teacher said to me, 'You've got to have a work/life balance. That's why I decide Saturdays are for me. I work all week, then I go to the football Saturday, and then spend all day Sunday planning and marking'. And he had this way about him, as if he'd just divulged the secret to a healthy work/life balance, and a happy, successful teaching career. I was gobsmacked. I thought to myself, what you've effectively just said, is that I'm about to start working a 6-day week for a salary way below that of the average graduate role[68] (again, it's not *about* the money. But this didn't scream work/life balance to me). I decided at that point that I would try to keep my hours (roughly) to that of a standard 40-hour week, and that no more than half of my holiday time would go towards schoolwork. Some teachers will almost brag about doing 70-hour weeks, but I am a strong believer that **happy teachers are good teachers**, and that burnt-out, stressed-out, teachers, can sometimes be the ones who falter. I get into work at 8 am each morning, and I try to be out the door by 5 pm. On occasions I'll be there later, sometimes I'll get out earlier. I try to take a half-hour break throughout the day (often this is the first thing lost to printing resources for the afternoon – but at the very least I try to give myself 10 minutes to eat my sandwiches), and I make a personal choice that once I am home in an evening, I am home, and not half watching the telly, half marking books. I believe I owe my family that much. Sometimes I can't stick to my plan, maybe there's a data deadline coming up and some marking just needs to be done; in that case, I'll do a later night at school. It's part of the job. But I, personally, would rather stay late and get that done, than take that home with me. You may differ, but make sure if you are taking work home, that you have a clear break between 'work time' and 'relaxation time' (such as doing marking in a different room, then going into the living room with a

---

[68] School Teachers' Review Body. (2018) *Twenty-Eighth Report – 2018: Executive Summary.* Available at:
https://assets.publishing.service.gov.uk/government/uploads/system/uploads/attachment_data/file/728384/CCS207_CCS0518679568-002_Executive_Summary_WEB_ACCESSIBLE.pdf

clear head, and with all your school-stuff put away, and out of mind, until the next day).

You may end up working more hours than a standard working week, especially to begin with. *Trust me*, I know the pressures we're under as teachers, so don't feel bad if you are spending the odd Saturday planning or marking. But try not to make this isn't *every* Saturday, and make sure you're spending a bit of time each day relaxing. You owe it to your mental health. Also, take advantage of those holidays. You might spend a week of a two-week holiday working, or the first three days of a one-week half-term. But that other half is an absolute perk of the job. If you're a traveller, travel. If you're a gamer, game. See friends, get outdoors. Sometimes this job will feel like it's sucking time away from you (and other times we can't wait to get into the classroom and start our days), so when you have got some free time, enjoy it! Your wellbeing is hugely important and something you need to actively take care of. We're in this profession to make positive changes to others' lives, but you need to also take care of yourself and make sure you don't forget your own needs.

Final Remarks

Have I managed to cover everything you'll need to know in your early teaching career in this guide? Not by a long way. I don't think any book can. Every school is different, every young person is different. The only way you can *really* become a high-quality, confident, teacher, and the only way you can really provide the best education and support for your particular group of students, is to get into a school and learn by doing. Teachers learn to teach in the classroom, and no guide will ever change that. What I hope I have been able to do is provide a little support, and summarise a few key things, that will help you along your journey. When you're really struggling for an idea for a starter, or an ice-breaker activity to use with a new class, or if you think you've heard a safeguarding concern and you're not sure what to do about it (**tell a DSL**, by the way), I hope this guide has been able to point you in the right direction.

Please don't ever forget that what you do is **incredible**. Most people could not do what you do. This became clearer than ever before during the Covid-19 lockdowns when parents had to start teaching their own children from home. Many stepped up and did as good a job as they could, some did an amazing job, but many struggled[69]. Struggled with one or two children. And I like to think, as a result of this, they grew a little extra appreciation for what we do day-in-day-out with classes of thirty or more. Teaching is a skill,

---

[69] Sellgren, K. (2020) Coronavirus: Home-schooling has been hell, say parents. *BBC*. Available at: https://www.bbc.co.uk/news/education-53319615

it's a difficult job, but it's also one of the most rewarding things, I believe, a person can do with their professional life. It's something that bleeds into our personal lives. There are not many jobs like it, and it takes a certain kind of person to do it. And when we do it, we change lives, and we change the world.

So, when you do next have a tough day (they will come, but they'll also pass), remember what an incredible thing you're doing, and think about the people you're doing it for. Remember the millions of positives that sprinkle themselves through our days and weeks- the look on a student's face when the concept you're teaching clicks and they finally understand, the courage it takes for a shy child to speak up and ask a question, or go further and take part in a school drama production, the surprise of a young person who's just done something they thought they'd never be able to do, pass an exam, score a goal in PE, or just make a new friend.

A lot of who we become as adults is shaped during our time at school, and by the examples people like teachers set for us. Many of us can think of teachers who inspired us, who, usually without knowing it, changed the course of our lives. For me, it was Dr Hartley. I probably wouldn't have gone on to study geography at university, and I almost certainly wouldn't be a teacher today, if it hadn't been for his lessons. We now, as teachers, will be that inspiration for a whole new generation of young people. It's a big responsibility. But like I said, this isn't like many other jobs.

I will leave you with this, a quote from Carl W. Buehner, which I think captures the essence of how much we can positively impact the young people we work with: '**They may forget what you said, but they will never forget how you made them feel**'.

For more regular teaching tips and advice, make sure to follow @HelpfulTeacher_ on Twitter.

References

Alexander, R. (2009) 'Towards a Comparative Pedagogy', in Cowen, R. and Kazamias, A. M. (eds) *International Handbook of Comparative Education*. Springer: London. pp. 923–942.

Ansari, A., Shepard, M., and Gottfried, M. (2022) School uniforms and student behavior: is there a link? *Early Childhood Research Quarterly*. 58 (1), p.278-286.

Bennett, T. (2017) *Creating a culture: how school leaders can optimise behaviour*. Available at: https://assets.publishing.service.gov.uk/government/uploads/system/uploads/attachment_data/file/602487/Tom_Bennett_Independent_Review_of_Behaviour_in_Schools.pdf

Bennett, T. (2020) *Running the Room*. John Catt Educational LTD: London.

Black, P. (2016) The role of assessment in pedagogy – And why validity matters. Ch.45, p. 725–739 in D. Wyse, L. Hayward & J. Pandya (eds.) *The Sage Handbook of curriculum, pedagogy and assessment*. Sage: London.

Brain Balance. (2022) *Normal Attention Span Expectations By Age*. Available at: https://www.brainbalancecenters.com/blog/normal-attention-span-expectations-by-age#:~:text=Childhood%20development%20experts%20generally%20say,focus%20on%20a%20given%20task

Caplin, M. and Childs, L., (2021) *Why you need to embed music into every lesson*. Available at: https://www.tes.com/magazine/teaching-learning/primary/why-you-need-embed-music-every-lesson

Chandler, L. K., & Dahlquist, C. M. (2015) *Functional assessment: Strategies to Prevent and Remediate Challenging Behavior*. 4th ed. Pearson: London.

Christodoulou, D. (2017) *Making Good Progress? The Future of Assessment for Learning*. Oxford University Press: Oxford.

Coombs, A., DeLuca, C., LaPointe-McEwan, D. and Chalas, A. (2018) Changing approaches to classroom assessment: An empirical study across teacher career stages. *Teaching and Teacher Education*. 71 (1), p.134-144.

Dabell, J. (2018) *Educational Super-Fad: The Madness Of Triple Marking*. Available at: https://www.teachertoolkit.co.uk/2018/05/06/educational-fad-4/

Department for Education. (2011) *Teachers' Standards: Overview*. Available at: https://assets.publishing.service.gov.uk/government/uploads/system/uploads/att achment_data/file/665522/Teachers_standard_information.pdf

Department of Education (2022) *Keeping children safe in education 2022*. Department of Education: London.

Department of Education. (2021) *Induction for early career teachers (England)*. Department of Education: London.

Department of Education. (2022) *Get into teaching: salaries and benefits*. Available at: https://getintoteaching.education.gov.uk/salaries-and-benefits

Earle, S. (2021) Principles and purposes of assessment in the classroom. *Impact*. (12), p. 20–23.

Education Endowment Foundation. (2021) *School uniform*. Available at: https://educationendowmentfoundation.org.uk/education-evidence/teaching-learning-toolkit/school-uniform

Education Executive. (2019) *Retention rate for teachers worsens*. Available at: https://edexec.co.uk/retention-rate-for-teachers-worsens/

Elliott, V., Randhawa, A., Ingram, J., Nelson-Addy, L., Griffin, C. and Baird, J.A. (2020). *Feedback: Practice Review*. London: Education Endowment Foundation.

Elliot, V., Baird, J., Hopfenbeck, T., Ingram, J., Thompson, I., Usher, N., Zantout, M., Richardson, J., Coleman, R. (2016). *A Marked Improvement?* London: Education Endowment Foundation.

Fiorella, L. (2020) 'The Science of Habit and Its Implications for Student Learning and Well-being'. *Educational Psychology Review*. 32 (1), pp. 603–625.

Gangwer, T. (2009) *Visual Impact, Visual Teaching: Using Images to Strengthen Learning.* 2nd edn. Corwin Press: Thousand Oaks, California.

Glenmoor and Winton Academies. (2018) *What is "No Hands up? @ GW?".* [PowerPoint presentation]. Available at: https://www.glenmoor.org.uk/Portals/2/No%20Hands%20up%20presentation.pd f?ver=2018-06-13-123859-243

Gotwals, A. and Cisterna, D. (2022) Formative assessment practice progressions for teacher preparation: A framework and illustrative case. *Teaching and Teacher Education.* 110 (1), p.103-120.

Gregory, K. (2011) The importance of employee satisfaction. *The Journal of the Division of Business & Information Management.* 5 (1), p. 29-37.

Hallam, S. (2015) *The Power of Music.* Music Education Council: London.

Hattie, J. (2009). *Visible Learning: A Synthesis of 800+ Meta-Analyses on Achievement.* London: Routledge.

HM Government. (2021) *Teachers' Standards.* Available at: https://www.gov.uk/government/publications/teachers-standards

HM Government. (2022) *Children with special educational needs and disabilities (SEND).* Available at: https://www.gov.uk/children-with-special-educational-needs

HM Government. (2022) *English proficiency: pupils with English as additional language.* Available at: https://www.gov.uk/government/publications/english-proficiency-pupils-with-english-as-additional-language

HM Government. (2022) *Pupil premium.* Available at: https://www.gov.uk/government/publications/pupil-premium/pupil-premium

HM Government. (2022) *School workforce in England.* Available at: https://explore-education-statistics.service.gov.uk/find-statistics/school-workforce-in-england#releaseHeadlines-dataBlock-1

HM Government. (2022) *Schools, pupils and their characteristics.* Available at: https://explore-education-statistics.service.gov.uk/find-statistics/school-pupils-and-their-characteristics

Johnson, B., and Bowman, H. (2021). *Dear Teacher*. Routledge: Abingdon-on-Thames.

Kippers, W., Wolterinck, C., Schildkamp, K., Poortman, C., and Visscher, A. (2018) Teachers' views on the use of assessment for learning and data-based decision making in classroom practice. *Teaching and Teacher Education*. 75 (3), p.199-213.

Koretz, D. (2017) *The Testing Charade: Pretending to Make Schools Better*. The University of Chicago Press: Chicago.

Kraft, M., and Dougherty, S., M. (2013) The effect of teacher-family communication on student engagement: Evidence from a randomized field experiment. *Journal of Research on Educational Effectiveness*. 6 (3), p. 199 – 222.

Larkey, S. (2015) *Reducing Anxiety and Increasing Participation with a NO HANDS UP Rule*. Available at: http://suelarkey.com.au/wp-content/uploads/2015/03/reduceanxiety.pdf

National Education Union (2018) *Teachers and Workload*. Available at: https://neu.org.uk/media/3136/view

National Education Union. (2019) *Classroom observations of NQTs*. Available at: https://neu.org.uk/advice/classroom-observations-nqts

National Education Union. (2020) *Guidance on classroom observation protocol in England*. Available at: https://neu.org.uk/advice/guidance-classroom-observation-protocol-england

National Education Union. (2021) *Feedback and marking*. Available at: https://neu.org.uk/advice/feedback-and-marking

Newport Academy. (2021) *Why Teens Need Rules: How Parents Can Support Both Independence and Structure*. Available at: https://www.newportacademy.com/resources/mental-health/why-teens-need-rules/

Newton, P., and Salvi, A. (2020) How Common Is Belief in the Learning Styles Neuromyth, and Does It Matter? A Pragmatic Systematic Review. *Frontiers in Education*. Available at: https://www.frontiersin.org/articles/10.3389/feduc.2020.602451/full

Northern, S. (2011) School uniform does not improve results – discuss. *The Guardian*. Available at: https://www.theguardian.com/education/2011/jan/18/school-uniform-results

Romer, D., Reyna, V., and Satterthwaite, T. (2017) Beyond stereotypes of adolescent risk taking: Placing the adolescent brain in developmental context. *Developmental Cognitive Neuroscience*. 27 (1), p.19-34.

Rosenshine, B. (2012) Principles of Instruction: Research-Based Strategies That All Teachers Should Know. *American Educator*. 39 (3), p 12-19.

Saloviita, T. (2013) Classroom Management and Loss of Time at the Lesson Start: A Preliminary Study. *European Journal of Educational Research*. 2 (4), p.167-170.

School Teachers' Review Body. (2018) *Twenty-Eighth Report – 2018: Executive Summary*. Available at:https://assets.publishing.service.gov.uk/government/uploads/system/uploads/attachment_data/file/728384/CCS207_CCS0518679568-002_Executive_Summary_WEB_ACCESSIBLE.pdf

Sellgren, K. (2020) Coronavirus: Home-schooling has been hell, say parents. *BBC*. Available at: https://www.bbc.co.uk/news/education-53319615

Shepherd, J. (2009) Pupil misbehaviour costs others a lesson a day. The *Guardian*. Available at: https://www.theguardian.com/education/2009/apr/14/pupil-misbehaviour-lesson-wasted

Smith. L., Todd. L., and Lang. K. (2017) Students' views on fairness in education: the importance of relational justice and stakes fairness. *Research Papers in Education*. 33 (3), p.336-353.

UK Parliament. (2022) *Education Act 1918*. Available at: https://www.parliament.uk/about/living-heritage/transformingsociety/parliament-and-the-first-world-war/legislation-and-acts-of-war/education-act-1918/

University of Birmingham (2018) *Lesson Plan Template*. University of Birmingham. Unpublished.

About the author

Alex Boyle, MA, BSc (Hons), has worked with young people in a variety of roles for the past decade, before first working as an unqualified teacher for a charity supporting adults with SEND in 2016. He attended the University of Birmingham's PGDipEd (Postgraduate Diploma in Secondary Education) programme in 2018 and gained his QTS (Qualified Teacher Status). He would return to the university in 2020 and earn his Master's Degree in Teaching Studies, focusing on how academic language is taught in the classroom and how teacher intervention can help in closing the vocabulary gap found amongst students.

He spent his first three years of teaching in mainstream secondary as a Geography teacher, and has since worked in a SEND secondary school, teaching just about every subject there is. On Twitter he can be found at @HelpfulTeacher_ offering regular tips and advice for new teachers.

Printed in Great Britain
by Amazon

26270604R00079